Connecting People

Discovering Peace and Power through Cultural Flexibility

by

Thomas S. Watson, Jr.

Lawrence W. Watson
Editor

Nuff Publications
Washington, DC, USA

1994

Dedicated to

The Almighty Creator of varying names and images
and my parents, Thomas S. and Geraldine W. Watson
and my Aunt Zora Fields Mitchum, who
shaped my early years of development.

Acknowledgements

I wish to acknowledge Willie Peter Sick for bringing my attention to the concept of cultural flexibility before we had a name for it and Wilbert Luck, Bennie Hadnott and my many other business partners for their continued interest in expanding my horizons through expanding the scope of Watson Rice & Company.

I am especially appreciative for Benjamin Day, our office manager's monumental administrative support and Ayanna Najuma, my publicist's energy and creativity in promoting my new career as a storyteller and inspirational speaker and my extended family and friends' invaluable advice and guidance in the reading and rereading that was required to produce this book.

Thanks to publisher, Paulette R. Bowles, for unwavering support and effective inspiration in keeping me motivated to finish this writing task; Michael Hunter, a most innovative and creative graphic designer and Edwin Brown Jr., an imaginative artist who captured the essence of our folktales.

Most especially I thank my children Kimberly A. Crawford, Timothy S. Watson and Andrew T. Watson who read and commented on the draft manuscripts showing immeasurable wisdom and insight.

Contents

Preface

People in all walks of life are talking about change. Economists discuss world economic changes. Politicians give speeches about global political changes and the forming of a new world order. Religious leaders preach about global and personal transformations in spiritualism, religion and personal fulfillment. Educators talk about changes in educational theory, goals and pedagogy. Journalists write about global, political, social and economic evolution. Many are reacting and responding to these changes and the pressures of change. Philosophers recognize that change is painful, even change that brings ultimate pleasure or ease.

My intention in writing this book is to introduce you to a different perspective on the changing world and its potential impact on your life. The folktales in this book are included to open your mind and attitude so that the intended message can be more easily received.

The introduction and the first chapter, personal change and the effects of technological advances, are linked. The second and third chapters are fictional narratives which have been written to begin to open your thinking to the possibilities for interpersonal communication which are not generally accepted or expected.

The fourth chapter outlines an approach to interpersonal communication which is based on a combination of good communication skills and genuine interest in people.

The fifth chapter offers two alternative futures which can be built using the leadership choices currently available. It suggests that it is now possible to shift from the global preoccupation with destruction and control of others to a new paradigm. The new paradigm acknowledges that access to information has intrinsic value and therefore information provides an alternative basis for power. It suggests that using information as a basis for power gives additional value to communication skills such as cultural flexibility, intuitive thought and persuasion.

The final chapter offers the changing South Africa as a living example of the possibilities inherent in adopting a new paradigm by focusing on the skills of cultural flexibility and intuitive thought.

The appendix provides definitions of terms, suggested reading lists, additional information on fellowships and other opportunities for expanding your personal growth.

The purpose of this book is not simply to promote cultural flexibility, but also to encourage people to pursue a higher level of personal development and a broader level of understanding of the world around them. The following concepts and stories should stimulate your thinking.

Introduction

Old Man and The Eagle

There once was an old man who had never seen an eagle. One day a magnificent eagle flew onto his window sill, and when he saw it, he exclaimed, "What an ugly creature!"

The man grabbed the eagle and pulled it into his house. "First, I'm going to fix that curved beak of yours." He used a file to remove the hook in the eagle's beak.

"Those claws are vicious looking," the old man said, as he clipped the eagle's claws until there was little left.

When he finished, the man said, "There, now you look better." He put the bird back on his open window sill and shooed it away. You can imagine how long the newly trimmed eagle lasted, defenseless in the world.

I originally heard this tale told by a well-known London based writer and lecturer, Idries Shah. I have since used it with many audiences. A moral of the story is: "Do not try to change what you do not understand." It is an idea that has become increasingly important to me as I tell stories and give speeches around the world.

In January 1991, I began using the speaker's podium to advocate cultural openness and curiosity about all people - what I have come to call cultural flexibility. Cultural flexibility is grease which lubricates the gears of our global society and allows diverse cultures of the world to live and work together. To date, my message has been well received and appreciated by people of all races in the United States, Europe, Bermuda, Mexico, the Caribbean and South Africa.

The concept is important to me because of what I have experienced and observed. As a private sector member of the U.S. Delegation to the General Agreement on Tariffs and Trade (GATT) negotiations, I witnessed how cultural flexibility helped a delegation to the GATT negotiations when the talks were in jeopardy. In December 1990 in Brussels, GATT talks were stalled by the European Community's recalcitrant position on agricultural subsidies. While others on the U.S. Delegation were talking among themselves and building frustrations, I connected with a group of European business leaders. These business leaders explained that many European business organizations supported the United States efforts to reduce or remove European subsidies on agricultural exports. I brought this information back to the U.S. team. After negotiations broke down, the U.S. Delegation held a press conference. The leader of our team used my findings to strengthen the U.S. position. Because I was able to meet and talk with leaders of European business groups who were not in the European government, our delegation leader knew that European business leaders employing more than 30 million workers were in support of reducing European agricultural subsidies. Cultural flexibility empowered me to get information which was not available to others on the U.S. Delegation.

Because cultural flexibility is an unfamiliar concept to many, I often use thought provoking stories and folktales to make it more understandable and believable. For example, a college professor told me of her personal transformation when I lectured at her university. She further confided that initially she did not want to hear my address. As a white tenured professor, she wondered what an African American man, from a firm she did not know, could possibly tell her. However, after hearing my address, she told me that she saw the people on her campus through new eyes. She did not realize that my stories allowed her to experience cultural flexibility in a way that was acceptable to her! It had not been me, but my stories that had moved her. This has been a common reaction to my speeches. Many minds are opened and transformed by the folktales I use.

Lessons from folklore are universal, handed down from older generations to the young who care to listen. The humor and wisdom of folktales can play significant roles in people's acceptance of each other as nations attempt to bridge differences of culture, race, gender and religion by connecting people in what is fast becoming an interdependent world.

Folklore has opened people in many ways, on many levels. Folktales explain nuances of human interaction and thereby add to the listener's experience base. This expanded experience base often opens new avenues to intuitive thinking, the "gut feeling" or instinct which is so necessary for effective leadership.

T. S. Watson, Jr.
December 1994
Washington, DC, USA

CHAPTER I

The Global Imperative for Change

Changes in the World

Changes in the political conditions and alignment of nations are bringing new economies and cultures to the forefront. South Africa now has the potential for great political and economic influence since the demise of apartheid and the election of President Nelson Mandela. Germany has reunited after more than forty years of division. The Union of Soviet Socialist Republics (USSR), once a superpower, has crumbled. The resulting independent states are struggling to help each other in establishing democracies and market economies.

Political, social and business environments have been changed by micro-chip and jet age technology. Oceans and distance no longer separate people. With jet airplanes, it is possible to travel to any part of the world in a day or two. Corporate executives hold worldwide meetings by video conference. Corporations encourage salespeople and technical workers to work from home, using electronic networks. Students of all ages learn new skills using long distance interactive video instruction. Across the globe, people exchange information, enjoy discussions and access research information on Internet, known as the Information Highway. Worldwide networks provide daily news updates via satellite. People fax messages to all parts of the globe in minutes. Modern technology is making us one interdependent world. It is breaking down barriers, bridging differences and bridging distances between companies and nations.

To foster competitiveness for themselves, nations are creating regional trading blocks and negotiating free trade agreements which encourage regional trading and stimulate regional economies. For example, the North American Free Trade Agreement (NAFTA) is giving Mexico additional power and visibility in the global marketplace. In fact, outgoing Mexican President Salinas is a leading contender to become the first president of the newly forming World Trade Organization (WTO). The European Union combines the economies of its twelve member nations into a powerful force, approximately twenty-five per cent of the global economy, which has greatly influenced world trade negotiations.

But as these nations combine economic strength to enhance their global competitiveness, technology is creating personal discomfort. Technology is blurring the borders between communities, nations and regions, allowing immigrants to stay connected to their homeland and making assimilation into their new culture less necessary. Earlier immigrants were cut off from their old world by distance and therefore had to assimilate into the new culture to find friends and establish roots. Their families eventually identified more with their new nation than the old homeland. Without this necessity for adaptation to the new, people are more inclined to cling to the old tribal, national or cultural ways.

Pressures from technology based changes are causing people to act more tribal than ever before. In *Global Paradoxes*, futurist John Naisbett explains that as companies and economies become more global their people act more tribal. An increasing divorce rate, job-related travel and job-related family moves are separating people from their family roots. The loss of easy identity with a family, community, state or nation makes them want to cling to tribal affiliations (nationality, race or ethnicity). They soothe their feelings of aloneness with a more fierce attachment to tribal or ethnic identity.

Recognizing that the world has changed and is still changing, it is important to acknowledge that the future of each person, company, community, city, region, and nation is inextricably interdependent with the rest of the world. Many cultures have economic strength and global influence. Nations must compromise and cooperate in situations where a few once dominated all others. For years the powerful nations or corporations of the western world were able to dominate all others. Many wanted to speak English and to emulate the management practices, mores and religions of the western world. As other nations come into political and economic power, this is less true. Today, skills in technology, management, business, politics or diplomacy are not enough. They must be enhanced by the skill of cultural flexibility to be effective in this changing world.

Cultural flexibility is the mental habit of overlooking superficial differences in physical appearance, personal beliefs, dietary preferences and life styles to find a basis for mutual respect and communication. It is a way of maintaining an open mind when dealing with unfamiliar conventions. It allows one to overcome the barriers or obstacles that inhibit the flow of communication between people. Cultural flexibility provides the willingness to understand, thus enabling one to define the milieu in which one is operating because it allows for appreciation of the other person's point of view and motivation. Cultural flexibility, if exercised, can influence how one is treated by others because of one's own demonstrated open-mindedness.

When combined with the mental habit of intuitive thinking (learning to listen to gut feelings), cultural flexibility will allow a leader to better understand and work within the changing marketplace, workplace, classroom or community where innovative leadership is required. This is explored further in the introduction to the Legend of Deacon Willie in Chapter Seven.

As an auditor, I traveled the world exploring the history and culture of each city I visited. Through my exploration of their folklore and historical stories, these communities came alive. I was often struck by similarities in the folktales. For example, there is a Persian story about Mullah Nasrudin stealing donkeys by using them to carry empty baskets across the Egyptian border. In the United States, it has become a joke about a factory worker stealing empty wheelbarrows from the Ford auto assembly plant in Detroit. Through folklore, it is possible to develop an appreciation and respect for other cultures.

Traveling nationally and internationally for years, I began to notice that I was received with more warmth and openness outside the United States than at home. Business and political leaders in Japan, Australia, Germany and many other nations welcomed me as an influential American. At home I had to continually fight negative stereotypes and prove that I was not "like the others". In discussions with Willie Peter Sick, a German veteran of Hitler's Army, I discovered why. He told me that Germans and others not only respect the accomplishments of African American professionals, they also find us more open, flexible and willing to respect them. Over a period of three years, he and I had worked together building an international network of middle-market companies. In the process, we became friends and exchanged information about our personal attitudes and feelings. This was the beginning of my discovery that people are beginning to value cultural flexibility.

As the people of the world intermingle, new opportunities will arise for many to reexamine and alter their opinions of others. Attitudes will be altered as more people learn to use cultural flexibility to reach out to new people, places and ideas.

Cultural Flexibility is Best Described by Example

1. Outside a Tokyo museum, a group of young Japanese girls on a school tour, asked to take my picture. After the photo session some of the girls wanted to rub my hands and touch my hair. They had never seen an African American person before. Some African American people might have been offended by their request, but I considered it genuine and

acquiesced. These innocent young grade school girls were reaching out for information in a perfectly natural way. They seemed pleased that I was willing and able to show them that I am not very different from them.

2. After a few days in Tokyo, the young Japanese woman who was my interpreter began asking questions about the life and treatment of African Americans in the United States. She did not believe what she had read in the papers and magazines. Since I was the first African American person with whom she had worked, it was important to provide her with clear answers to her questions.

She wanted to know if there were any white people in the neighborhood where I live. *There are.* She asked if I find work more difficult. *It is not. My education has prepared me well for the career I have chosen.* She asked if is it hard for me to advance and earn respect from my peers? *It is. I generally have to prove that I am more capable than other African Americans who have come before me.* She asked if people are killed often in my neighborhood. *I was raised in a middleclass home. I do not know of a killing which happened in any neighborhood where I have lived, including childhood homes.*

The discussion with me may have opened her eyes to the culture and capabilities of African Americans. She will be able to pass her newfound knowledge on to her Japanese friends.

These are examples of cultural flexibility. Such episodes provide opportunities to open oneself to people of other cultures, to exchange information about personal values, or to adapt to new cultural environments.

Not long ago, the Cold War pitted superpowers against one another in dangerous games of chess. Today, ethnic conflict is destroying lives, communities, institutions and nations. Right now, there are three hundred 'ethnic cleansings', 310 civil wars, twenty-five religious conflicts. Some people claim the time of foretold biblical upheaval is at hand. These conflicts, which show that cultural superiority and arrogance still control the passions of some people, do not bode well for the future of our world.

A Need for Cultural Awareness

Some recent political leaders have not learned. A language instructor for the U.S. State Department told me of an experience she had with a former Secretary of State. She was correcting the language in a speech he was preparing to deliver in Spanish, when he exclaimed, "I have a graduate degree from Harvard and have been a prominent political leader for many years. What makes you think you can tell me what to say?" She replied, "Mr. Secretary, I am not telling you what to say. I am just telling you that what you want to say is not said that way in Spanish." She says that this has been typical of the resistance she must overcome while teaching Spanish or Portuguese to U.S. political officials.

Americans expect visitors from other countries to speak English whenever they live and work in an American office or factory. For example, a quality control specialist for a mid-western manufacturing plant complains, "I hate it when they hire Mexicans. It's hard enough to hear what someone's sayin' on the plant floor with all those machines and freezers going. You add a foreign accent or, worse yet, put someone who doesn't speak English well and you might have a very dangerous situation. Someone could misunderstand a warning or some special instruction and have their whole hand cut off before they even knew what was happening..."

Another example: A secretary from Tennessee adds, "I can't stand to have to talk to foreigners on the phone. There's this one guy. He's from Korea or someplace. I can't understand a word he says. He's talking English, but it's like he can't separate his l's from his r's. Every time he calls I have to have him repeat his message over and over. Not only am I tired of it, but I think he thinks I'm stupid."

"What is the benefit of diversity, anyway? Why not simply employ people who look and act just like me? The Germans do it. The Japanese do it. Why not in my American company?" This is a challenge many corporate leaders must answer.

Cultural Flexibility in Corporate Leadership

Generally U.S. executives and managers have not needed cultural flexibility before now. During the Industrial Age the United States dominated world markets. The foundations for international business were the English language, the U.S. dollar and the values of western civilization.

Newfound economic power in the Middle East, Japan, South East Asia, Mexico and Southern Africa has diffused global influence to many cultural regions of the world. Micro-chip technology and jet air travel are making all parts of the globe accessible to the people of most nations. We are all closer together now in this new global marketplace. We have become interdependent people with interdependent economies. Therefore, attitudes must change. U.S. businesses must find culturally flexible executives and managers to help them adapt to this new global environment.

In Germany, a mostly homogeneous population is aging at an increasing rate. The German economy and that of the entire European Union (current name for the European Community) is beginning to depend on an underclass of laborers imported from the Third World.

While it is true that Japanese firms emphasize the promotion and advancement of their Japanese personnel, the resulting strain on the life style of the average couple reduced the birth rate as the Japanese economy has grown. Their 14 to 17 hour work days leave little time for family responsibilities. So naturally, with labor demand increasing, and the population of under eighteen year olds in Japan declining, Japan has begun to import workers.

If statistical patterns hold, the most homogeneous of populations will be forced to integrate. Gradual aging of indigenous populations will create a need to import a more youthful work force. Host nations must find ways to accept and integrate these immigrants into their population to avoid internal friction between cultures.

What kinds of problems will these immigrant populations create for the host nations? Presently, the immigrant population of Japan is at a disadvantage culturally and socially because of ethnocentrism and racism in Japan. Many Koreans, Iranians, and Chinese who work and live in Japan endure daily discrimination by the Japanese. Japan's ethnic minorities find themselves discriminated against in housing, job promotion and marriages. This is an undesirable state of affairs for all concerned.

However, people dependent upon outside laborers cannot treat those laborers with disdain and prevent them from advancement without a severe backlash. Moreover, a population accustomed to the comforts of a homogeneous workplace, school and market-place, will have to adapt their thinking and acting in order to peacefully co-exist with their foreign neighbors. They will have to learn to communicate with them, to understand their behavior, habits and customs and to relate to them as well as they relate to each other. Sounds simple, but for a homogeneous and ethnocentric population these changes could be world shattering.

The risks are great. For example, plantation owners in the Southeast United States lost their economic stability as a result of cultural arrogance toward their African slaves. This arrogance resulted in an inflexibility which remains even after a devastating

Civil War. The resultant turmoil is still reverberating through the United States of America.

Another example is treatment of Burakumin in Japan. Burakumin cannot be distinguished by physical appearance, religion, education or any other identifiable characteristic. They are truly Japanese - born, raised, educated, employed, indoctrinated in the Japanese systems and culture. However, they are put at the bottom of the Japanese pecking order because their forefathers, in the early days of feudal society, worked in socially unacceptable trades. They included executioners, meat processors, workers in leather, actors, maintenance workers and trash collectors. Buraku families are subjected to discrimination for generations. Detective agencies thrive on illegal research into the ancestry of potential employees or marriage partners. Books listing the Buraku families by address and occupation are widely sold and used. Communities of Burakumin are regularly scoured for scapegoats when perpetrators of crimes cannot be found.

Feminization of the Workforce

In Japan and the industrialized European nations, women are slowly entering the workforce. Although more than fifty percent of the population, women have historically been discouraged from working in the factories and offices. The United States has begun to embrace the female workforce and has enacted laws for their protection against discriminatory acts and harassment. Feminization of the workforce adds a dimension to both labor and executive levels of U.S. businesses. Feminine priorities are becoming relevant in corporate decision making. Feminine concerns are becoming the companies' concern. Feminine intuition is becoming a tool of advertising departments and feminine perspectives are often considered in establishing policies and laws.

In addition to the feminization of the workforce, there is also the introduction of racial and political minorities into the decision-making level of North American commerce.

Race and Perception in the United States

Many still remember the United Negro College Fund (UNCF) television advertisement featuring a young black boy wearing a Superman suit and looking at a reflection in the mirror. The reflection of himself that he imagines is a tall white man with blue eyes and blond hair. He will never look like that! His impossible dream undermines his self-esteem and his career potential.

However, many African American men and women today have learned to build a foundation for accomplishment and have earned respect without becoming white. Cultural flexibility provided the foundation that they needed to bridge the realities of their culture and physical appearance with the expectations of the dominant culture. This bridge is a basis for building mutual respect, clear communication and commonly acceptable goals between African Americans and members of the dominant U.S. culture.

For the past thirty years, bridges were being built between African Americans and the dominant U.S. culture. During the same time, European immigrants were assimilating into the mainstream. Although European immigrants had to learn the U.S. culture and find ways to assimilate, they did not need to build permanent bridges for communication and cooperation. To the contrary, African Americans needed the permanent bridge of cultural flexibility because their differences in physical appearance will not go away.

Where African Americans have been able to make their imprint, they have revolutionized thinking and standards of the industry. By employing cultural flexibility they have revitalized policies and practices. Many have risen to the top of their professions through hard work, dogged determination and persistence. Bill Cosby changed the standard for television situation comedy by showing an entertaining functional family unit, as an African American family the group gained nearly universal acceptance. Spike Lee added words to the common vocabulary, including "wannabe", which is often used by newspaper and magazine writers to describe aspiring politicians and actors, among others. This list must include athletes who raised the standards for their sports: Jesse Owens, Wilt Chamberlain, Kareem Abdul Jabar, Jim Brown, and the many similar young athletes of today's games.

African Americans are a source of culturally flexible leadership. Affirmative action and set-aside government procurement programs have given African Americans the opportunity to develop technical and management skills. Integration into a society and culture dominated by people of European mores and practices forced African Americans and others to learn another culture as well. They developed the skill of cultural flexibility as a method of understanding this new culture. Now African American corporate executives, entrepreneurs, political and religious leaders are prepared to use the skills and talents they have developed. These skills are most valuable and best appreciated from a global perspective.

Examples of Culturally Flexible Executives

Paula Cholmondeley (a Jamaican born woman) was hired by Faxon, a $400 million company founded in 1881, to restructure and improve its international division. Four years later she had increased international sales by 30% and increased U.S. jobs by 15%. As a member of the Faxon executive team, she helped to develop a global management focus.

In the process, she taught a sixty year old Japanese man to become a more effective planner; restructured Faxon's European operation (allowing the acquisition of an old line German competitor) and improved client relationships in South America. She was well respected by her Faxon colleagues and staff in North America and abroad.

Another example is an experience that my firm (Watson Rice) had in a joint project with a major international accounting firm. The two firms were engaged to develop a computer-based accounting system for a program run by the Egyptian government. A few months into the project, they were facing termination by the Egyptian government. After some discussion between senior management of Watson Rice and the other firm, on site project management was shifted from the major firm to Watson Rice. The job ended with a written commendation from the Egyptian government for a job well done! The only change was in the leadership of the project team. The same people did the work. But the on-site team leaders were people who had more cultural compassion for the Egyptian client.

Marcus Griffith (a Guyanese entrepreneur) and his personal care products company, Hairlox, is another example. When he had been in the personal care products business for more than twenty years, Marcus Griffith discovered markets for his products in other parts of the world. He began exporting personal care products that were originally designed for African Americans. After just a few years of culturally flexible business dealings, he now exports his products to more than twenty-five countries, to markets in Europe, the Middle East, South America, the Caribbean and Africa.

Hairlox had to find ways of getting paid and shipping products in environments that are generally hostile to U.S. products and businesses. Hairlox executives have been creative, flexible and respectful of the values of other nations. These qualities have brought the company continued success abroad, during a time when Hairlox faced stiff competition and declining sales in North America.

Another example comes from my personal experience in developing an international trade symposium, Export 89. As Co-Chairman of Export 89, I led an American delegation that organized the first Small Business International Trade Congress. Our European partners said that success of our effort resulted, in large measure, from the cultural flexibility of our leader. We developed this program (which has since evolved into a multinational trade association) without major political support or large investments of money. Export 89 opened the door for American and European small and medium enterprises (SMEs) to operate in the combined economies of the United States, Canada and the European Community. This is a combined economy of $10 trillion and 600 million consumers.

The Latin Connection

In addition to the blessing of African American culture, North America benefits from a strong and growing Latin population that is diverse and sophisticated. This American population is made up of Mexicans, Cubans, Puerto Ricans and people from every Latin American country. These diverse groups emigrated to the United States sometimes fleeing oppression in their own countries, but always bringing a valuable perspective to their new country.

Juan Ortiz, a Mexican engineer, who makes his home in Los Angeles, sums it up this way, "We came from Mexico in 1932 to find a better way of life. My father didn't speak English and my mother was always sick from drinking the water here. But now, my children can attend a private Catholic school where my beliefs are shared by them and their little comrades.

It is wonderful here because if one part of the country is not to your liking, you can move to another state and it is as though you are in another country. Each state has its own identity, its own character. There is no one America.

America is where you find it. And you get out of it what you put into it..."

Still, the Latin experience has not been without some hardship. While Latin Americans were never slaves in the United States and never were owned as property, stereotyping and discrimination have left an impression of Latin Americans that fuels their desire to overcome and flourish.

Miguel, an unemployed youth living in Boston, explains his dilemma this way. "They think you are a thief. All the time, no matter what you do they think you are carrying a knife and looking for some 'white chica' to grab and rape. You can't judge people like that. This stereotyping thing is what holds me back."

In response to, or maybe because of, such stereotyping, Miguel has developed a reluctance to get up in the morning to look for work. He says he feels hopeless and that he may leave the United States to work in Canada. If not Canada, there is always the unspoken possibility of turning to a criminal life, thereby fulfilling the stereotype and decreasing the overall potential of his community. Equity in treatment and the absence of stereotypes are important for the potential of individuals to be turned from fighting the system to more productive pursuits.

In Japan and Europe, the historic homogeneity and the emerging need to replenish spent labor resources will lead to their eventual acculturation with the Third World. However, where the most violent and unproductive aspects of these transitions are history in the United States, the rest of the world is just beginning the transition. As members of the dominant U.S. culture encourage the ambitions and accomplishments of its minorities, the United States can gain and maintain a competitive advantage in world markets. To realize this opportunity, minds must be opened to new possibilities and novel approaches.

Changing environments require changes in leaders. The world is not using its full human capability. No nation will remain world competitive without participation from all its cultural groups, races and both genders. Having observed how the destinies of millions of people are affected by the signatures of a few individuals on a treaty, I am committed to using the wisdom of folktales and stories to encourage people to re-educate themselves.

In the Christian tradition, Jesus was a storyteller whose parables and stories made such a lasting impression on people that his teachings became renowned as a true way to enlightened coexistence with others. Mohammed's wisdom, in Islamic tradition, was learned through stories and parables about his life. While Jesus' and Mohammed's methods and their wisdom are sometimes overlooked in modern times, it is my hope that this book will renew interest in these basic truths.

CHAPTER II

Connection: *A Fictional Narrative*

This fictional narrative is intended to challenge stereotypes in a thought provoking manner. It should prick your psyche and help you to begin an exploration of the concept of cultural flexibility.

Through a set of shared circumstances two men of different physical appearances and cultural backgrounds learn how much they have in common.

Jim, a white man, small of stature but nattily dressed, made his way up the busy street, unconcerned by the squalor of people sleeping in doorways and alcoves around him. Purposefully averting his gaze, he walked briskly holding his breath against the smell of unwashed people and blankets.

Suddenly, from behind a concrete pillar, a homeless beggar approached.

"Gimme' a dolla', man!" he demands waving an outstretched hand.

"What?"

"Gimme a dolla, man. I need sumpin' to eat," Shouts the toothless beggar.

Jim looked harried. He increased his pace averting his eyes from the demanding pan-handler.

Finally passing him by, Jim heaved a sigh of relief. The homeless man cursed him and approached his next target with the same demanding entreaty.

The next passerby, a tall, heavy-set African American man, replied..."Man, get a job."

At the corner, the white man paused to let traffic pass. Larry, the large African American man, approached. Still behind Jim, Larry said, "Man, I hate those guys."

Emboldened by the seeming camaraderie expressed by the tall stranger, Jim replied, "My thoughts exactly."

"You know, if those guys would put half the energy they put into getting drunk and high into getting some work done, they'd have money," exclaimed Larry.

Surprised, Jim replied, "I agree."

"I blame the liberal welfare state." said Larry. Curious, the white man asked, "What do you mean?"

"Well, it's like this," Larry said, suddenly energized.

"I work for my money. I have never used food stamps or collected welfare. I don't steal. I don't smoke crack. I don't waste my money in bars or on whores. If those guys could just clean up their act a little bit, they could live at least as well as I do. But instead of getting up in the morning and trying to find something productive to do, they sleep until noon, start drinking as soon as they get up and don't stop until they pass out again at night. They should be incarcerated where they could dry out and get straight. But no! The government would rather give 'em a check. Now that welfare check is not really enough to live well, but it gives them enough to stay alive. And since they can do that with no effort, that's all they do."

"I've never met someone like you who felt the way you do," Jim said.

"You must not know very many working black men," Larry replied.

"None who speak their minds the way you do."

"Well, let me tell you something. My name is Larry. Black conservatism is much more widespread than many white people would think. It's just that in the liberal media, the only African Americans they show you are on welfare or being arrested for committing a crime. Most of us are hardworking, church going people who believe in families, raise our children and earn a living."

Larry continued, "What white people should understand is that the true judge of people is the content of their character, not the color of their skin. But knowledge of character can only be realized when we down-play our differences and allow ourselves to discover common concerns and issues upon which we can agree."

"Interesting." said Jim. "Look. I don't really have anything to do right now. If you don't mind, why don't I buy us a couple beers and we could talk some more."

"Can't. I'm on the job and I've already wasted enough time today. Why don't you give me your card and maybe someday I'll call you."

"Okay." Jim produced a business card and handed it to Larry. "Do you have a card?"

"Here." Larry said handing him an embossed business card. "Just ask for Larry." Larry stuck Jim's card in his shirt pocket. Later while at his desk he produced the card and read it for the first time.

It read: Dewey, Cheetum & Howe, Certified Public Accountants. Jim Scrumpt, Managing Partner and CEO.

Larry regarded it coolly and placed it in the top drawer of his desk.

Days later, he retrieved the card and called the number at the bottom of it. A prim white sounding female voice answered the phone.

"Mr. Scrumpt. Please."

"May I tell him who is calling?" the voice said.

"You may tell him it's Larry."

"May I say what this is regarding?"

"He'll know."

A few minutes passed. Before long the familiar voice answered,

"Hello?"

"Mr. Scrumpt. How are you? This is Larry." He said. "We met two days ago on the street corner. Remember, I am the African American man you talked with briefly on the street after I commented on the bum who was pestering you for money. You invited me to call you when I had the time."

"I remember."

"Well. I've got this friend. He's a good guy but he's having a hard time starting his accounting careeer. He graduated from a major university with a nationally renowned accounting school. He was in the Navy for six years...stationed on a submarine, I think. I'm not sure. Anyway, I was wondering if someone in your position could meet him and maybe instruct him on starting a career in accounting. I'm sure you've seen 'em come and go. All he really needs is some career counseling. Not a job per se, however, I'm sure he would be appreciative for any leads you might provide."

"I'd be happy to meet your friend, Larry. Why don't we do it over lunch?" Scrumpt said. "How does the twenty-third sound?"

"The twenty-third it is. When and where?"

They confirmed a lunch date for the three of them.

On the appointed day, Larry and his friend met at Larry's office for a final briefing.

After checking him out and making sure he was ready, Larry took his friend, Dominic, to the appointed restaurant. In the lobby, they met Scrumpt who greeted the two warmly.

At the table, the menus were returned to the waiter and lunch and cocktails ordered. Larry let Dominic make the first move.

After some perfunctory life histories, Scrumpt abruptly turned to Larry and asked, "Do you mind if I am completely honest here?"

"I would prefer it," said Larry, calmly.

"When we spoke on the phone two days ago, it happened to be at a time when I was remembering what you said about the quality of a person's character. At the time I agreed to this lunch, I expected your friend to be African American."

"Is it a problem that he isn't?" asked Larry.

"No," said Scrumpt, "But I have to admit it is a surprise."

"Well, it's like this. Dominic has been a friend of mine for many years. And now he needs help. There was a time when I needed help. Even though he didn't have to, he came through for me. This is an opportunity to help him get his career started. It makes no difference to me that he is white. The important thing is that for many years, he has been a good friend."

"Your attitude is as refreshing as it is unexpected," said Scrumpt.

"I found you and Dominic intriguing during our brief meeting. I'm having a party at my home next weekend. I was wondering if you'd be interested in coming?"

"When and where?"

"I'll see that you get an invitation if you give me your mailing address again."

"Sure. It is...."

Two weeks later, Larry and his wife were dressed in their finest. They drove to the party at an exclusive high rise apartment building. The invitation had instructions for them to proceed to the 26th floor. They arrived just in time to watch a beautiful sunset. From the balcony of the apartment they recognized the private yachts on the lake. They watched the yachts' lights twinkling on as twilight became darkness over the city.

Larry turned to find Jim Scrumpt approaching. He cordially introduced his wife Jenny, and Larry introduced them to his wife Karen. And thus began a lasting friendship between two families of very different ethnic and cultural backgrounds.

From a casual meeting on a city street two men have discovered their potential for bridging cultural, racial and other artificial boundaries which exist between them. They and their wives are learning to understand and respect each other. There are often opportunities to overlook superficial differences and find a basis for mutual respect and communication.

CHAPTER III

Women's Work:
A Fictional Narrative

This fictional narrative provides a beginning hint to the universal appeal and timelessness of folklore. It also is intended to challenge stereotypes about women, Native Americans, Muslims and the Middle East. It shows women in power and their responsibility for shaping their own destinies. It also hints of benefits for upwardly mobile professionals to remain connected to family, history and ancestry - connecting people.

An upwardly mobile Native American woman executive is offered an opportunity to use her unique perspective to assist an ambitious Muslim politician. She is pleasantly surprised to find that she and this visionary prime minister have much in common.

On a hot, muggy Washington day, the fumes from the congested traffic left visible films of residue on her front windshield. As Trelinka watched the unmoving cars blocking the intersection, her mind drifted to a far away past.

In her vision, she was a small girl again, living in the North Dakota trailer park with her people, the Dakota Sioux. On cold winter days, she tramped across the hard packed snow to greet her grandfather's pickup truck when it lumbered into the short drive-path in front of the trailer.

Her grandmother, a short, squat woman with long grey braids tied with leather chords would hunker in their tiny kitchen and entertain her and her mother for hours with gossip, tales of courage, and folktales just before bedtime.

Thinking back to those days made her feel safe and cool. She remembered how the barely-insulated trailer let the frigid north wind chill her until the heat from her body and her grandmother's soft voice warmed the sheets and pillows beneath the thick cotton blankets.

Her grandmother spoke in the traditional language of the Dakota Sioux, for she was utterly disdainful of English and all things "American". She lit her corncob pipe, and warmed her hard old feet under the blanket where Trelinka's own tiny toes pressed against cool sheets.

Trelinka wondered why she was remembering her grandmother telling this particular trickster tale.

The Trickster and His Bundle of Songs

One day on their annual journey north, a flock of ducks stopped to rest beside a small lake. The ducks enjoyed the rest from flying and were playing in the water.

One of the ducks noticed a strange looking creature coming toward them, carrying a huge load. As the creature got closer, she saw that it was a little old man with a large bag.

By the time the creature got close, all the ducks had stopped playing. The old man sat down. He was the trickster, Old Man Coyote in disguise! And he was hungry.

"What do you have there?" asked the duck who first saw Old Man Coyote.

"Where?" said the old man. Coyote was up to his old tricks. He was hungry. The ducks would make a good meal.

"That bundle, on your shoulder," said another duck. They all scrambled out of the water to see.

"Oh, this!" said Coyote. "It is only a bundle of songs." He stretched out on the ground to rest.

This aroused the ducks' curiosity, which was what Coyote wanted. They pleaded, "Sing us a song from your bundle!"

Coyote sat up and smiled. Then he built a small tepee with sticks from the ground. For a roof, he pulled dry grass from the bundle and attached it to the top of the tepee.

"Now come inside this shelter, and I will sing you a song." Coyote coaxed.

The ducks crowded into the tepee. It was a tight fit. But they all made it. Coyote stood by the door, outside.

He began to sing, "Dance with your eyes closed. Enjoy the beautiful music."

The ducks listened to the song, keeping their eyes closed. As he sang, he grabbed the ducks one by one and shoved them into the bag. They were so busy dancing that they did not even have a chance to quack for help.

The ducks inside the tepee did not notice that their friends were missing. They kept their eyes closed and enjoyed the music.

When only a few ducks were left, the duck who had first seen the old man felt that something was wrong. She opened her eyes just a little and saw Coyote grab one of the ducks and shove him into a large, moving bag.

She opened her eyes all the way in terror. "Fly, fly" she cried, "He will kill us all."

The remaining ducks all opened their eyes wide and rose up with a huge clamor and quacking. The tepee fell to the ground and the few remaining ducks escaped.

"You have tricked us," they cried as they flew off.

With this story, Trelinka's grandmother was warning her to beware of the Trickster, who in all his forms, continues to try to capture the spirit of women.

A shrill siren awakens Trelinka from her daydream. "Enough is enough," Trelinka growls into the steering wheel. She wheels onto the far lane, and executes a dangerous u-turn into oncoming traffic. Horns blare. She continues on her way, down the next block and around the unmoving obstruction.

Finally at her office, frustrated because she is more than an hour late, she slides past the receptionist and into her office where her assistants are already lined up vying for attention.

"Trelinka" said her most ardent assistant, Lucille, a tall, thin woman who was determined to move into a management position with the firm. "You are late for your 9 o'clock appointment with the State Department's Mr. Salinger. He's called three times from his car saying the thruway is backed up because a truck ran over somebody's dog. A car loaded with children who saw the accident, sideswiped another truck loaded with ammoniated gas. It is leaking all over the beltway at the Greenbelt exit.

Anyway...He's gonna' be late." She said wrapping up the news flash. "Want some coffee?"

"Love some," Trelinka replied. "Next?"

"You're booked on a British Airways flight to Persiastan with a layover in London. You'll be staying at the Hussain Hilton. Your reservations are already made. You are permitted to take two bags with you, but no lap top computers are allowed on the flight. You know the European paranoia about terrorists is especially acute in London.

Lucille continued, "You will be briefed Thursday morning. They'll schedule the time and place once you get there. And your doctor's appointment has been moved up from Thursday to today as you requested. May I ask what this meeting is about?"

"As soon as I know, I'll consider telling you," said Trelinka smiling. While she did have some idea what was going on, the specifics were just as much a mystery to her as they were to Lucille. But she decided when she accepted the assignment, the only way to assure herself the promotion she wanted was not to shirk from assignments just because they were on the other side of the world.

Trelinka's office was on the top floor of the World Trade Center in Virginia. She was the highest ranking woman and the only Native American executive with Andersen & Ernst, the international communications consulting firm.

For seven years she had been training to be vice-president for international marketing strategies. To train for the position she learned to speak seven languages including Arabic and Farsi.

As the only Arabic speaker in her division, she was a natural selection for the summons from the first female prime minister of Persiastan.

Now, her bags packed, her shots, visa and passport in order, she drove out to Dulles International Airport ready to board the plane for the other side of the world.

Twenty-four hours, four meals and one airport hotel later she landed in Persiastan at the Muhammad Ali International Airport. She was greeted by Mr. Bhutto, the prime minister's courteous personal representative, who whisked her through customs and ushered her into a long limousine. Seated in back, she was overwhelmed by her bone weariness. The smooth ride and the extended flight contributed to her unceremoniously succumbing to jet lag in a quiet and dignified sleep.

The next day, she awoke to the brilliant sunlight of the Persiastani morning. In the bathroom of her hotel room she found a huge marble tub in which she luxuriated the grime of twenty-eight hours of travel from her stiff, brown body.

An hour later she was dressed and seated in the restaurant of the Hilton sipping coffee and enjoying the complimentary sweet rice. She was to meet an envoy from the prime minister's office who would brief her on etiquette and security for her meeting with the enigmatic Prime Minister Ahminah Ali.

By five o'clock that evening, her briefing long since completed, she was tired of waiting and longed to go out of the hotel to soak up some of the local color she could observe from her balcony. But etiquette demanded, according to her new friend, Mr. Bhutto, that she make herself available at a moment's notice for summoning to the government building for an audience with the prime minister.

At last...at 11 pm the phone rang. She picked up the receiver and a prim voice in heavily accented English said, "Please hold for the prime minister."

Despite her preparations, Trelinka trembled slightly at the thought. But before she could react to the tension, a smooth female voice on the other line said, "Trelinka Wolf. It is good to finally speak with you.

"I am sorry we could not get together today. But if you are a night person like me, maybe we can meet shortly, say about twenty minutes?"

"I would like that." Trelinka replied.

"Good," said Prime Minister Ali. "My driver will meet you at the Hilton. You may want to bring a change of clothes. It is not uncommon for my special guests to stay the night. There is a place for you and we will do our best to make you comfortable. Again,

I apologize for today but please be my guest this evening. I am anxious to meet you."

"I will be ready..." Trelinka said.

"Good. I will see you shortly."

Twelve minutes later a Persian driver pulled in front of the main doors of the Hilton. Trelinka walked out, identified herself, and entered the car when the driver opened the door for her.

Soon the limousine crept up the driveway of the Prime Minister's House. Inside, she waited to be received. After a few minutes, Mr. Bhutto came out to meet Trelinka. He escorted her into the private office of Prime Minister Ali.

"I am so glad Andersen & Ernst sent you for this job," the prime minister said.

"First, I know you speak our native language. But we'll use English for now. Have a fig newton?"

Trelinka looked at the plate. The treats looked tempting. She couldn't resist.

" I developed a taste for these in the States. How I miss those days."

"Harvard, right?" asked Trelinka.

"Class of '79," replied the prime minister. The two women spent the next few minutes exchanging memories of Harvard and their very different career paths.

"Well...enough about the past. Let's discuss the future and why you're here," the prime minister reluctantly ended the reminiscing.

"I want to appoint two women to my Cabinet. The party leaders are going to scream bloody murder and they'll probably put another bomb in my car. But these women are capable and I think its time we took our rightful role in government.

Persiastan is a Muslim nation with cultural traditions which deny rights that women in your own country take for granted. There are only a few women professionals here, compared to thousands in the United States. In some parts of this country, women are not valued as highly as men.

I contacted Andersen & Ernst because I need the power of a major international firm for what I want to do. In this term, I intend to change my country and maybe the entire Muslim world. I intend to show women are equal to men in every practical way. And you are going to help me do that."

"But Prime Minister, the women's movement in countries like the United States took decades to accomplish these goals to which you aspire."

"Perhaps, but they didn't have the advantages we have to-day...namely a woman prime minister, the full power of our national government, my world-wide image and my network of influential friends."

"All right. A campaign?"

"More than a campaign. A full fledged revision of national history and Islamic history. Are you familiar with the Quran? Let me tell you how this whole situation started and you tell me whether or not we can change this thing from front to back, top to bottom.

"At the time of Prophet Mohammed the Arab nations were treating women as chattel. A woman had no rights except those which were granted to her by her father or husband. She could not inherit property. Women did not even have the right to claim their own personal earnings.

In the Quran, Muslims were given a clear message that women were to be considered equal to men in all regards, including the right to own property, hold earned income and present legal testimony. In some respects these rights were expressed in terms of the rights of men. These have been interpreted by some of today's men as giving them the right to dominate, own or control women in ways that are contradictory to the intentions of the Quran and the instructions of Prophet Mohammed. It is time for us to correct these misconceptions. I want to end miscarriages of justice by weak men who would prefer to hold women in subjugation so that they will not need to compete with, understand or respect them.

The Quran's Surah (Book) Four, titled "The Women, Chapter Two" lays forth the rights of women and the duties of men in regards to women. It clearly says that men as the stronger gender have the responsibility to respect and protect women. But in matters of property, legal action, inheritance and earnings women have rights as do men."

"But how will you persuade men to relinquish their superiority?" queried Trelinka.

"Our campaign will not be directed toward men," answered Prime Minister Ali. "That would be a waste of valuable resources," she continued, "My ambition is to inform the women of the Islamic world of their power: the power of awareness and positive action! You see, when I was a young girl my aunt used to tell me a story about a Trickster who beguiled some ducks. She used this story to warn me to beware of the Trickster in all his forms who tries to capture the spirit of women like me."

Trelinka's smile said it all. She was going to like working with this woman. But more importantly, She understood why her grandmother's story came to her in the traffic a few days and thousands of miles ago.

Their respect for family ancestry and folklore helps these two very different professional women to connect across cultural and occupational lines.

CHAPTER IV

Steps in Using Cultural Flexibility

Introduction

There is not one best way to develop cultural flexibility any more than there is a best way to drive or walk from one place to another. In walking or driving, there is a fastest way or a shortest way. But the best way is determined by the skills, interests and experiences of the driver, walker or learner. For example, the best way to walk home from school on a sunny autumn day may be through the woods if you enjoy looking at the many colored leaves. There are easier and faster ways to get home. But this will be the best way for you on this particular day.

Outlined are seven steps which can be used to understand and introduce cultural flexibility into your life as a mental habit. With continual practice of these steps, you can develop the habit of thinking in a culturally flexible manner.

Step 1.   Build Your Admiration and Respect for the Other Person.

Find something you truly respect in the other person or group. This may not always come easily. Unless you learn to listen carefully, you may misunderstand what people are telling you. Or you may be disappointed like the yogi whom Deacon Willie met.

Saved His Life

Driving west from the Mississippi Delta in his new Ford Bronco, Deacon Willie passed near a strange looking building, at the entrance of which a hermit was sitting. The hermit had an air of abstraction and calm, and Willie thought that he would make some sort of contact with him.

"Surely," the deacon thought, "a devout philosopher like me must have something in common with this saintly individual."

"I am a yogi," said the anchorite, in answer to Deacon Willie's questions, "and I am dedicated to the service of all living things, especially birds and fish."

"Please allow me to join you," said Willie, "for, as I had expected, we have something in common. I am strongly attracted to your sentiments, because a fish once saved my life."

"How pleasurably remarkable!", said the yogi, "I shall be delighted to admit you to our company. For all my years of devotion to the cause of animals, I have never yet been privileged to attain such intimate communication with them as you. Saved your life! This amply substantiates our doctrine that all the animal kingdom is inter-linked."

So Willie sat with the yogi for some weeks, contemplating his navel and learning various curious gymnastics.

At length the yogi said to him, "If you feel able, now that we are better acquainted, to communicate to me your supreme experience with the life saving fish, I would be more than honored."

"I am not sure about that", said Willie, "Now that I have heard more of your ideas."

But the yogi pressed him, with tears in his eyes, calling him "Master" and rubbing his forehead in the dust before him.

"Very well, if you insist," said Willie, "though I am not quite sure whether you are ready, for the revelation I have to make. The fish certainly saved my life. I was on the verge of starvation when I caught it. It provided me with food for three days."

In looking for something admirable in others, you sometimes find the unexpected.

Life is not always easy nor always what one might expect. But occasionally when all seems lost, someone or some series of events restores one's faith in humanity and our Creator. How I got to a recent speech is one such series of events.

Traveling On Faith

Upon arriving at my office, I found things unusually hectic. But I was able to use my short time in the office well. Later, I went out to meet a delegation of Senegalese who were visiting the United States. After this meeting I did a talk show interview at a local radio station, talking about international, political and economic policy.

When I came out of the radio station, it was raining. Because I was wearing a rain coat and hat, I arrived at our office building garage without getting very wet. I took off my coat and hat, put my traveling hand bag on top of the car and put my coat in the trunk. I then got into the car and drove over thirty miles to Dulles Airport in pouring rain, arriving at about 8:15 pm. When I got out of the car and retrieved my luggage from the trunk, I looked for my hand bag. It was not in the car. It was not in the trunk. My plane ticket, money, driver's license, credit cards, bank machine cards, business cards and the expense check for the trip were inside the handbag.

I then began the ordeal of finding a way to get to Hollywood, Florida, in time for the next morning's speech. There was a flight leaving at 10:30 pm, delayed from 9:15. It had seats available, but how could I buy a ticket without a credit card or driver's license?

The answer was provided by my son, Timothy, who was a student in the School of Business and Industry at Florida A & M University. He prepaid my ticket using his credit card. With much help from an airline employee at the ticket counter, I was able to get the ticket just in time for the plane. The ticketing agent worked overtime, keeping her husband and a young child waiting, to help me retrieve the ticket. For this I am sincerely appreciative.

Once landed in Florida, the ordeal was not complete. I still had to get from the airport to the hotel, to check into the hotel and to order a meal at one in the morning, with no money or identification. The taxi driver who took me from the airport to the hotel was an understanding and cooperative man. He waited patiently while I, without identification, persuaded the hotel clerk to cash a personal check.

The hotel clerk was most accommodating. She found the convention manager who had invited me to speak and got an approval to cash my check. She gave me enough cash to pay the taxi driver and purchase a light snack from room service. The next day the convention manager lent me enough money to pay for a taxi back to the airport.

The Almighty Creator's hand can be seen in many places and at many times. My message from the speaker's platform has forever changed because of this experience. That evening I was touched by many people, none of them African Americans. All were kind, understanding and helpful beyond the requirements of their position. As a result, I now include an evangelical message in my speeches about international business and trade policy. The evangelical message is that we are all God's creatures. Therefore, we must learn to look past superficial differences of color, clothing, language and culture to find the beauty in each of us, whom God has created.

Step 2.   Show your respect in a clear and visible manner.

If you learn to show admiration as effectively as David's father did, in the following urban folktale, your influence may turn out to be very far reaching and long lasting.

Little League

It was David's last Little League season. Like every other year, he and his father came to every game arm in arm. They would walk up to the front row of the bleachers where his father would sit while David played occasionally; but mostly he sat on the bench.

With two weeks left in the season, young David's father died. David came to the next game alone. He approached the coach saying, "Coach, my father died last week. You may not understand why, but it is important that I play in this game today. Please let me start."

The coach having sympathy for the newly orphaned boy agreed to let David start the game at center field. David played a marvelous game. He had three hits, stole four bases and was catching balls in the outfield that no one else could have caught. With the score tied 2 to 2 in the ninth inning, David hit a triple. His hit drove in the winning run. His team won the game. He was this game's most valuable player.

When the game was over the coach greeted David on the field. "That was a marvelous game you played today. But you have never, ever played like that before. Why today?"

"Well coach," said David, "You know that my father died last week. But you may not have realized that Dad was blind. Today is the first game he has ever seen me play."

David was motivated by his father's admiration and respect even more after his father died.

The strategy of the Hoopoe when confronted with an unreasonable demand from his king, is an example of the value and potential benefits of showing genuine respect for admirable characteristics of another.

Hoopoe's Wisdom

King Solomon was known throughout the world for his wisdom. He could command the winds and animals to come whenever he called them. He even knew the language of every creature on earth.

One summer day, King Solomon asked his wife what gift she would like for her upcoming birthday.

"I would like something that no other queen on earth had ever had. Build me a palace of bird beaks," she demanded.

Out of personal pride and love for his wife, Solomon promised, "You shall have a palace of bird beaks."

Then King Solomon ordered all the birds of the world to come to his palace, prepared to give up their beaks. Soon thousands of birds filled the sky, beating their wings and swooping down to the palace. They all came--the powerful eagle, the small hummingbird, the bluebird, the woodpecker and every bird on earth. They were not pleased to give up their beaks. But, there was nothing else they could do. Soon every bird had come to the palace except Hoopoe, a tiny bird with colorful feathers and a pointed beak. This made the king angry.

"Catch Hoopoe and bring him here!" he shouted to his servants. "He will be punished for not obeying the king!"

At last Hoopoe appeared before the king.

"Why have you kept me waiting?" King Solomon demanded.

"Oh wise King Solomon, please do not be angry with me," said Hoopoe. "I have been flying to the ends of the earth seeking wisdom, so that I may serve you well. Punish me if you must, but first give me a chance to show the wisdom I have gained. Let me ask you three riddles. If you can answer correctly, then do whatever you want with me. But if there is one that you cannot answer, spare my life."

The other birds were shocked that a bird dared to bargain with the king. But King Solomon admired this bold gesture and accepted the challenge. He said, "Ask your riddles."

So Hoopoe spoke. "This is the first riddle. Who is it who was never born and has never died?"

The king did not even pause to think.

"The Almighty Creator, Lord of the worlds," he said at once. As he spoke, King Solomon thought, God created all animals and mankind to be free.

Hoopoe continued. "Here is the second riddle. What water never rises from the ground and never falls from the sky?"

King Solomon's smile showed that he knew the answer. "A tear that falls from an eye that cries with sadness." As he finished Solomon saw all those birds stretched out before him, waiting sadly for their beaks to be cut off. He was saddened. A tear came to his eye.

Now suddenly, it occurred to Solomon that building a palace of bird beaks was a foolish thing.

Hoopoe spoke again with a slight tremble, for there was only one riddle left, only one more chance to be saved.

"What is delicate enough to put food in a baby's mouth, yet strong enough to bore holes in wood?"

It did not take King Solomon long to reply. "Why, a bird's beak, of course!" he answered. Looking around at that great gathering of birds, he realized how very precious the birds' beaks were to them.

Hoopoe bowed. "You have answered my three riddles. Punish me as you will."

But the king was smiling. "Dear Hoopoe," he announced in a loud voice, so that all the birds could hear, "I am known for wisdom, yet you have shown me that a king sometimes must check his actions to avoid making a mistake. I have decided not to build a palace of bird beaks. For your wisdom, you will be rewarded," said King Solomon. He had the royal jeweler make a crown for Hoopoe. When the crown was finished, King Solomon himself placed it upon the head of Hoopoe.

To this day, Hoopoe wears a crown on its forehead, to remind all who see it of the reward King Solomon granted for the wisdom which saved the birds' beaks.

Wisdom takes many forms and generates many types of rewards. Hoopoe's display of genuine respect for King Solomon's wisdom was a wise action.

Step 3.   Find Things In Common.

You have a lot of information about the other person or group. They have experienced your genuine admiration for something about them. Now you can easily identify things about you which they can respect. However, the process need not be as dramatic as the experience of a father and son who went to the big city hospital.

Father and Son at the Hospital

A father and son were living in a small town when the son got very sick. The local physicians and hospital staff could not identify the son's ailment. So his father took him to the city for an examination and treatment. They checked into a hotel across the street from the hospital, then went into the hospital for the son's examination.

Upon examination, the medical staff decided that the son needed an immediate operation. However, in preparation for surgery, the anesthesiologist gave the son too much anesthesia. It was going to kill him.

The head surgeon came out to the waiting room and told the father. "We are sorry," said the surgeon, "but you will have to reconcile yourself to the fact that your son will die. We have given him too much anesthesia and it is going to kill him."

The father pondered for a minute and then replied, "Maybe so, Doctor. But you and your colleagues will have to reconcile yourselves to the fact that my son and I have different values than you. To demonstrate how different we are, I will go back to the hotel where we checked in, open our suitcase, take out the pistol we brought with us and load it. Then I will come back to this hospital and hide behind the bushes outside the physicians' entrance. If my son is all right, I will come out and all will be well. But if he should die, I will come out and shoot each of you, one by one."

The father got his gun and hid behind the bushes just as he had promised.

The son awoke the next morning, properly revived with a bevy of physicians and nurses crowded around his bed. He has lived a healthy life for many years since the incident.

But, his father had to raise the level of risk for the physicians and nurses before the hospital and medical staff would properly address a problem that they had caused. When their lives were at risk along with the life of the son, they found a solution to the medical problems.

In this case the one compelling thing that the family and the medical staff had in common was their risk of death. However, in most cases it is possible to find common traits and interests which will bind people together rather than force resolution to an unfortunate confrontation.

Your experience can be more like these two women who discovered that they have quite a lot in common even though one would not think so at first glance.

At a luncheon sponsored by the International Consortium for Governmental Financial Management, Ayanna Najuma, my publicist and the Consortium's Executive Director were seated next to each other for the meal before my speech. To look at them you would find it surprising that this fortyish African American woman from the Southwest and the much older white woman from Maryland have so much in common. They found each other's company delightful. They discovered that they are graduates of the same university, thirty years apart.

The comparisons of past and present drew them together. They both love dolls and as adults, have kept up with the dolls they enjoyed as children. They both knit. They enjoy the sense of accomplishment and the beauty of knitting.

A little curiosity about people will reveal much to respect, admire and find in common with them. As you find things in common, it is often easy to evolve a friendship, business alliance or other practical relationship.

Step 4.   <u>**Show Enthusiasm for Common Traits, Interests and Experiences.**</u>

In some cases the things you learn from another person will stretch your imagination and sense of reality as much as the turtle was stretched by its discussion with a man.

A Man Greets A Turtle on the Road

While walking through the woods one day a man saw a turtle and for no apparent reason the man spoke to it. "Hello turtle," he said.

The turtle could talk. It responded, "Hello, who and what are you?"

" I am a man," he replied, "And I am standing on legs and feet which I use to move around quite rapidly."

"That is amazing," the turtle replied, "Is there anything else unusual about you?"

"Yes, there is a difference in the way we use our houses. You have your house on your back."

"Yes, yes, all turtles carry their houses on their back."

"Well, we men have many houses and move about from one to another at will."

"Quite amazing, is there anything else unusual about you?"

"Yes, you know a leaf?"

"Yes, yes all turtles know about leaves."

"Well, a man can make marks on a leaf, pass it to another man who can then give it to a woman. The woman can look at the marks and know what the first man was thinking."

"Now I know what you are. You are a liar!" exclaimed the turtle.

The turtle was not able to understand the man's descriptions of walking, entering buildings and writing because its frame of reference was too narrow. You may run into people like this, but their frame of reference should not stop you from connecting with them. You may have to first give them some examples closer to their personal experiences so that you build their trust and their ability to identify with you.

Step 5. Once Common Interests Are Explored, You Can Then Reveal Something about Yourself Which You Know the Other Will Respect and Admire.

You have built a level of comfort which should allow the other person to demonstrate admiration and respect for you. However, your new friend may not see your actions any more clearly than the young boy who spent a day by the side of the road with Deacon Willie.

Deacon Willie's Roadside Example

A young boy joins Deacon Willie at the side of the road leading into their village thinking, "I will spend the day with this wise man and learn something of value from his instruction and actions."

Shortly after they sat down, a man came up to them and asked, "Old man, do you live in this village?"

"Why do you ask?" Deacon Willie replied.

"I am a salesman," answered the visitor, "and my company has offered me a promotion if I relocate to your town and cover the adjoining territory. I want to know what type of people I will be working with if I accept the offer."

"What are the people like where you come from?" asked Willie.

"Oh, my neighbors and co-workers are wonderful people," answered the visitor. "They are warm, caring people who look out for the best interest of others as well as themselves."

"You will find the same type of people in our town," Deacon Willie assured the visitor.

A little while after the visitor left, another man came walking down the road. He also stopped to greet Deacon Willie and his young companion.

"Say old man," frowned the new visitor, "do you live in this town?"

"Yes," replied the deacon, "Why do you ask?"

"Well, I have been offered a promotion. They want me to move to your town to run the local plant. I want to know what kind of people I will be working and living with in this town."

"What are people like where you come from?" asked Willie.

"Oh, they are mean, competitive and self-centered people. Not one of them would lift a finger to help another unless there was some immediate and obvious benefit to himself."

"Well, I am afraid that you will find the same kind of people in our village," warned Deacon Willie.

When the second visitor had left, the young boy turned to Deacon Willie and exclaimed, "I came out here to spend the day with you because I thought I would learn from your words and example. All I have learned is that you are a liar!"

"I am sorry to have disappointed you," consoled Willie, "But tell me, why do you think I am a liar?"

"You told the first visitor that the people of our village are nice caring people. But you told the second visitor that our people are mean and self-centered. We cannot be both!" The young boy was puzzled and frustrated.

"Console yourself my young friend," the deacon said warmly, "What I told those men is that people will reflect what they put forth. People will treat each man as they expect to be treated."

Deacon Willie not only taught the young boy a lesson in human nature he also guided the prospective immigrants to his town in a manner which encouraged the open-minded culturally flexible salesman but discouraged the mean-spirited culturally arrogant plant manager.

Step 6 .   Receive Their Respect.

Once cultural flexibility is developed, it can aid in building and receiving respect in a variety of ways. One example is in giving time and attention as the country doctor does in this tale.

You Need Oranges

A long time ago, a young man decided that he wanted to become a physician. But there were no medical schools in his small town. So he asked a respected and loved local physician to accept him as an apprentice. The physician agreed. After three years the young man was growing impatient.

"Doctor, I have worked for you three years. It is time I had a practice of my own. Let me handle the next patient."

"Son, I don't think you are ready," replied the physician, "But you can try to cure that old man coming down the walkway right now. He needs to add oranges to his diet to cure his malady."

The young apprentice greeted the man and invited him into the examining room. Before the man could get settled on the examining table, the apprentice blurted out, "You need oranges. The only thing wrong with you is that you need to add oranges to your daily diet." The patient was offended. He got down from the examining table and left the doctor's office in a huff.

"Doctor, what happened?", asked the puzzled young man.

"I could explain it to you, but you would not understand. When another patient comes in with the same malady, I will show you."

It was two weeks before another patient came in who also needed to add oranges to her diet, but eventually a woman arrived with the same illness.

"Come in Mrs. Shah," said the doctor guiding the patient into the examining room. "You are looking quite pale today. Let me examine you carefully."

The doctor used tools of the trade to look into Mrs. Shah's eyes, ears and throat. Then while observing her gait and posture the doctor mumbled, "Mrs. Shah, I think you need to add some citrus fruit to your diet. But what kind will be most effective? Lemon? No, that would be too sour. Grapefruit? No, not quite right. I've got it. Oranges would be just the thing! If you add oranges to your daily diet for the next two weeks, your problem will be solved."

"Oh, thank you doctor!" exclaimed Mrs. Shah. She left the examining office smiling and went to the payment window to willingly pay a very large bill.

"I still don't get it," complained the young apprentice, "My patient needed oranges. I told him he needed oranges. But it just made him angry. Your patient needed oranges. You told her she needed oranges. She was not only happy with your diagnosis. She paid a very large bill with a smile. What happened?"

"What you must learn, my young apprentice, is that your patient not only needed oranges, he needed time!" The wizened physician said with a smile.

Another way of receiving admiration and respect is demonstrated in the unorthodox behavior of Deacon Willie when he was invited to preach to a learned congregation.

The Sermon

One day while Deacon Willie was visiting in his wife's home town, the local church asked him to preach the following Sunday. Willie agreed. When Sunday came, Deacon Willie walked through the congregation, mounted the pulpit and exclaimed to the waiting crowd, "Who of you knows of that which I am about to speak?" The people did not know Willie. They had no idea what he might talk about. No one said a word.

"Well," exclaimed Willie, "I haven't time for such stupid people!" He got down from the pulpit and went home.

The church elders were shocked, but because of Deacon Willie's reputation as a wise and learned man they were determined that their congregation hear some of his wisdom. They invited him to preach again the following Sunday. He agreed.

When Sunday came, the deacon again walked pompously through the congregation, mounted the pulpit and again asked, "Who of you knows of that which I am about to speak?" The people remembered what had happened last week. So most of them said, "I do."

"Well," said Deacon Willie, "If you already know what I am going to say, why should I bother to say it?" He got down from the pulpit and went home.

The church elders were frustrated by Willie's actions but remained determined that their congregation hear some of his wisdom. They invited him to preach again the following Sunday. He agreed.

When Sunday came, Deacon Willie again walked pompously through the congregation, mounted the pulpit and again asked the same question he had posed the two previous weeks. The congregation thought they were ready. Half of them said, "We do." The other half said, "We don't."

"Great," said Willie, "Those of you who know, tell those of you who don't know." He got down from the pulpit and went home.

You may be constantly surprised by others once you are open to learning about them in a culturally flexible way.

I sat at the table across from a short, stocky "union man" during one series of international trade briefings held by the Department of Commerce. This man's constant stare made me watch him. As he continued to watch me it began to make me feel uneasy. I was very conscious of being the only African American person in this briefing. And this man looked like someone who might question why I was there. At the first refreshment break, Joe, the union man, reached across the table and said, "You are Tom Watson, the Chairman of Watson Rice. I heard you speak some time ago and was wondering if you would be willing to come to my union to address our leadership on trade issues."

Joe is one of the many people who taught me about cultural flexibility, just by his attitudes and actions. I had reacted to his stare with the knee-jerk reaction of many African American men in such a setting. What I was thinking was not on Joe's mind at all.

His invitation demonstrated to me that I should be open to attention from others regardless of their physical appearance.

Step 7.   **Use Your Common Interest to Bond with the Other Party.**

A connection built on mutual interest creates the ability to build trusting relationships which will allow each party to act more like the brothers in the following story.

Brothers Who Inherit a Farm

Two brothers inherited a farm. In the first year, they tilled the field together. They planted the crops together. They tended the crops together. And they finally harvested the crops together.

The night they finished the harvest, the younger brother could not sleep. After tossing and turning until two in the morning, he finally sat up on the side of his bed mumbling to himself, "This is not right. It just is not right! My brother has a wife, three children, a house note and a car note. He certainly needs more money than I." So he got up, put on his clothes and went out to his barn. He took a substantial part of his share of the crop and put it in his brother's barn. Then he felt better, went back home, took off his clothes and slept soundly.

Thirty minutes after he fell asleep, his older brother awoke with a start. He looked over to be sure that he did not awaken his wife. Then sat up on the side of his bed, thinking to himself, "This is not right. It just is not right. My younger brother does not have the comforts of family life. He is still finding himself. He certainly needs more money than I." So he put on his clothes and went out to his barn. He took a substantial share of what was in his barn and put it in his brother's barn.

These brothers continued to do this year after year, each year amazed that they had as much as they started with.

In strong partnerships where the partners understand that their interests are interdependent, they do not lose by looking out for their partner's welfare in addition to their own. When more people learn to do this by habit, they will begin the building of a better world attitude.

CHAPTER V

Intuitive Thought

Introduction

In dealing with people or the myriad of information (some fact and some fiction presented as facts) thrust upon us by changing technological platforms, we cannot rely on intellect alone. TV, newspapers and other media provide impressions of other people and places which cannot be disproved without direct experience. However, upon meeting a person or group of people, well-honed intuition can sometimes override conditioning to allow you to see them as they are rather than as others want you to see them.

There are two kinds of intuitive thought which are useful in the context of this discussion. One kind of intuitive thought is the unexplainable feeling that proves to be correct. Most people have had a feeling that they should do something or avoid something else. Although they could not prove logically why the feeling was correct, when they follow the hunch all goes well.

Another kind of intuitive thought results from withdrawing your mind from a perplexing problem and letting the answer come to you. Most people have had the experience of working on a problem, gathering more and more information but finding no solution. After a good night's sleep or a relaxing game of golf, the answer arises from our subconscious without any logical connection to the prior effort. This answer is invariably closer to the perfect answer than any previously considered.

These are processes of intuitive thought. They are part of the life experiences of most people. They have little basis in logic, but have clear basis in truth. We have found them to be correct, even if not comfortable for our rational educational training and culture.

A Mental Exercise

I am a CPA and MBA, deeply trained in logical and rational thought. Several years ago, I began using an exercise when leading strategic planning exercises. This exercise was designed to demonstrate how much of our intuitive thought has been educated out. You may want to see if you can still think outside of normal educative conventions. The numbers on the next page are arranged in a very specific order. Use a pencil and paper to figure out what order they are in.

8　5　4　9　1　7　6　3　2　0

5　5

4　　　4

9　　　　　9

1　　　　　　　1

7　　　　　　　　　7

6　　　　　　　　　　　6

3　　　　　　　　　　　　　3

2　　　　　　　　　　　　　　　2

0　　　　　　　　　　　　　　　　　0

The numbers are arranged in alphabetical order, using their written form in English, (eg., eight, five, four, nine, one, seven, six, three, two and zero). In groups of mature adults with business or engineering education, fewer than ten out of several thousand were able to get the correct answer. However, children in grade school classes almost always got the correct answer in very little time. The mental flexibility which is required to consider that the numbers are in alphabetical order has been educated out of most adults. The notable exception, in my use of this example, has been adults who are fluent in languages with varying character bases. They have generally done as well as the young children. That is to say that people who are fluent in writing and speaking Arabic, Farsi, Mandarin Chinese, or Japanese as well as English have been able to figure out the correct answer to this puzzle. They may have been required to rebuild their intuitive thinking before they could master the very different languages.

Intuition can often override prejudices and biases. Intuitive thought, the combined use of intellect and emotions, must become an integral part of everyday life. This can only become a personal reality when we are able to throw off the shackles put upon us by modern educational pedagogy and instructional theory. **The following stories can become tools for your use in moving beyond a slavish attachment to logic as the sole basis for intelligent thought.**

Girl in Park

A young girl wandered away from home at night. Lost in the park surrounded by ominous shadows she could not identify, strange noises that made her spin and start, the girl began to cry. Then the moon came out from behind the clouds. It was a full moon. Its shower of shimmering light rained down upon the girl, who raised her head as the shimmering light arranged itself into a series of steps floating up through the trees.

The girl went up the steps. With each step she took, she became lighter and lighter, until she had to hold on to the steps to keep from floating away. She continued to climb. Her curiosity finally made her wonder how high she was. When she looked down at the park, the height frightened her. Again she began to cry. She let go of the steps and floated into the sky, above the clouds.

Now the girl felt no fear at all. Because the whole world was hers. It curved below her, shining bits and patches. The girl could see it all. She could see the good places and the bad. She knew, without anyone telling her, that she could go any place she pleases. She just looks for the light and off she goes.

The girl's experience opened her intuition to connect with her world in a much broader way.

The legend of Deacon Willie presents a mythical explanation of the current emphasis on logic as the sole basis of intellect and education in the western world.

The Legend of Deacon Willie

A certain crafty villain was entrusted with the education of a number of orphans. Instead of teaching them how to learn, he told them that they already had the skills they needed. Then he insisted upon their doing some things and not doing others. Thus he kept most of them blindly subject to his direction. He never revealed that his original commission had been to teach them to teach themselves. When these children grew up he noticed that some had detached themselves from his authority despite all his efforts. Others remained bound to it.

The villain was then entrusted with a second school of orphans. From these he did not directly demand obedience and respect. Instead he enslaved them to his will by telling them that learning to think logically was the sole aim of education, appealing to their self pride. He never let the children guess that intuition was an alternative to the choice between emotions and intellect. Because intuition could be overcome or blurred by either of these, he always dismissed its appearance as irrelevant, coincidence or guess work.

Some of the children in the second school of orphans suspected that certain miraculous aspects of life did not fit into his fragmentary pattern and asked him if there was something else. He told one group of questioners, "Certainly not. Such a notion is superstitious. Do not put any value on coincidence." To another group he said, "Yes, there is more to life than you managed to collect under my direction". But he took care that the two groups did not compare notes and so realize that he had given two contradictory answers.

When the children reported inexplicable events to the villain, he dismissed them as having no scientific relevance. He knew that without considering intuition the children would never escape from the invisible net in which he had bound them. The intuitive knowledge of secrets excluded from their education could be gained only when they were in a certain harmony of mind with the emotions. So he taught them to ignore variations in their mental condition. Once they discovered that powers of comprehension vary from hour to hour, they might guess how much he had concealed from them. His training confused them, so they were willing to think along the logical lines that he had prepared for them.

The children whom this villain had misled in his first school had now grown up. Since he had let them come nearer to understanding the true nature of life, certain casual remarks that they made to members of the second school disturbed their faith in scientific truth. So he hastily gathered those of the first school who still remained loyal to him and sent them out to preach incomprehensible doctrines purporting to explain the hidden mechanism of life. Then he directed the attention of the second school to these teachers saying, "Listen carefully, but never fail to use your intellect." The intellectual children soon found that there was nothing to be learned from these doctrines.

So many different ways of thought were current that it was often said, "I cannot trust anyone. I must find out myself by the exercise of my intellect." The old villain who had bred all this confusion thrived on it like a mad man rejoicing in deeds of violence. His cult of the intellect encouraged egotism and discord. To those who still felt an inner uncertainty, a sense of incompleteness or a hankering for something whole and true he said, "Distract your minds by ambition." He taught them to covet honors, money, possessions, sexual conquests and to immerse themselves in hobbies and diversions of all kinds.

The fragmentary view of life forced on mankind by the villain was now accepted. The few people who tried to point out the truth were thought insane and were therefore refuted by the old argument, "If what you say is true, then prove it to us logically."

Nevertheless the tradition of intuitive thought passed on delivered by direct succession from an ancient sage to one of his descendants. The descendant searched the world to find the man who would carry the knowledge, namely the incomparable Mullah Nasrudin. Thereupon, the teaching was brought to the attention of the children who had been misled. Mullah Nasrudin broke out of the net which had been cast by the old villain. Nasrudin passed on these teachings to his North American cousin, Deacon Willie, and thus, spread enlighten-

ment to the Western World. Study the experiences of Deacon Willie. Let them become a part of your consciousness. Let them teach you to see the world through different eyes.

As with any legend, this tale appears to have combined fact (a description of the evolution of western education) with the fictional villain, orphans and a convoluted teaching system. Examine for yourself, not the question of truth or fiction, but the completeness or lack in your own education.

Stories from Deacon Willie and other folktales are included in this book as vehicles to transmit the essence of cultural flexibility and intuitive thinking to you, the readers. They are folktales which have been used as teaching tools for many years.

CHAPTER VI

Alternate Futures

Introduction

Here is another reason why the world needs cultural flexibility in its leaders. Power is shifting to those who control information. An example of how control of information translates into physical power or authority is seen in the following story of Queen Shahrazad. Because of this power shift and the needs created by the changes in technological platforms described earlier, people will choose between two alternate futures: they can continue to pursue the personal need for confrontation and dominance, as described in the story about the father and son at the hospital (Chapter Four, Step Three), or they can choose to find mutual interests and pursue enlightened self-interest by looking out for others, as did the two brothers who inherited the farm (Chapter Four, Step Seven).

The purpose of this chapter is to make you think about the world's future from a different viewpoint. In the shift to an Information Age, changes in technological platforms are changing our world. These changes include:

1. computer access, through Internet, the Information Highway;

2. jet and other air travel which a person can use to travel from one location to another, anywhere in the world in a matter of hours. It has been estimated that within forty-eight hours you can go to any place on the globe using jets and helicopters and other modes of transportation;

3. transmission of messages over thousands of miles in seconds via telephones and fax machines;

4. changes in the method and speed of communication because of improved satellite communications, radio, television, interactive video technology; and

5. cyber-learning for language training which allows a student to put on goggles, listen to a recording and quickly become fluent in another language.

New technological platforms are changing our access to information and thereby changing lives. Today an employee of a major corporation can use electronic mail to communicate directly with the company chairman and vice versa. President Clinton and Vice President Gore are accessible to millions of electronic mail users across the nation, on *America Online*. Major publications such as *Newsweek* and *The Wall Street Journal* are available in electronic versions. President Reagan was regarded as the Great Communicator. But now we are presented with Bill Clinton's Video Town Meetings, which bring his message directly to the people through television. AT&T is advertising technology which allows students and teachers to be miles apart but still interact directly using video conference technology. Subways are using smart cards which deduct fares from toll cards as riders enter or exit the system. Computer programs like *LotusNotes* facilitate global design teams who communicate directly online over fiber optic cables. Home shopping networks allow people to shop and buy wide varieties of goods using television, telephone and credit card systems. These technological changes have changed our view of leaders and they have changed our values. Think about how these changes have altered your values.

These changes in technological platforms are changing leadership styles; leaders' roles and personal philosophies. Philosophical changes include not only increased attendance at religious services but also a curiosity about others. Today more people are willing to understand the beliefs and practices of other religions. There is a re-emergence of interest in metaphysics, new interest in the environment and a willingness to accept responsibility for the world's supply of water, land and air.

Technology is changing the numbers and nationalities of the people we meet, the places we visit, the food we eat and the cultural experiences we enjoy. Access to information through the *Internet* has become a popular topic of conversation these days. Writers are doing research online without leaving their writing desks. Researchers, scientists, politicians and others are using this new access to information to communicate, research and experience life in ways not dreamed about just a few years ago. Technology is bringing people closer together and forcing them to acknowledge differences in beliefs, cultures and ways of communicating.

How we relate to these differences in people will determine our future. We must be careful not to become like the old man who saw an eagle on his window sill, whom we met in the preface of this book.

Dominance Must Be Replaced By Persuasion

This reminds me of the message in the story for *1001 Arabian Nights*. Each morning the young queen would tell the king the beginning of an intriguing story. But sunrise would come before she could finish. Although she was to be beheaded that morning as the king had done for each preceding wife, she was spared because the king wanted to hear the end of the story. She would complete the previous day's story and then begin another, stopping at an enticing part each sunrise. By the end of her collection of tales, she was with child and the king spared her life in order for her to nurse his son. They lived happily ever after. This is how their relationship began.

Queen Shahrazad

There was once was a King named Shahriyar. His Queen was the disappointment of his life. One day he discovered that, in spite of her sweet words and smiles, she had been for many months sharing her favors with one of their servants and conspiring to have him killed. King Shahriyar's rage took hold of him. In his fury, he killed his Queen with his own hand.

He vowed, "Never again will a wife of mine deceive me!"

He decided that he would marry beautiful young maidens at will. But the morning after their wedding night he would have his new wife beheaded.

For some time he kept to his plan. After a while, there was hardly a beautiful young girl left in the kingdom. Indeed there were soon only the two daughters of his Grand Vizier.

When the King next said that he wanted a wife, the Grand Vizier told him that there were no more maidens to be had. At this, the King became furious and swore that if the Vizier did not immediately bring him a young and beautiful maiden, he would be beheaded at once. When he heard that, and saw the fury of the King, the Vizier returned sadly to his house.

His elder daughter was a lovely and wise girl named Shahrazad. When Shahrazad saw her father's sad face and noticed that he would eat nothing, but sat apparently weighed down with misery, she said:

"Why are you so sad, Father?"

At first the Vizier would tell her nothing. But when she persisted, he told her about the King's anger, and that he was sad because the King intended to kill him the very next day.

"Father, let me marry this King!" said Shahrazad.

For a long time the Grand Vizier would not be persuaded, but at last he agreed to rely on her guile. Before they left she asked that her younger sister, Dunyazad come with her. Her father agreed.

Only Shahrazad herself kept up her courage and no tears fell from her great dark eyes. But her father was almost dead with grief as, he brought her to the palace.

In an outer room Shahrazad left her younger sister. As she did so, she said earnestly:

"Dear sister, I will need your help! Tomorrow morning I am going to ask the King to allow you to be admitted to the inner rooms. An hour before dawn you must come in as if you meant to tell me goodby. But do not leave immediately. Instead present a cup of delicious sherbet to the King and another cup to me. Then say: "Tell me, as you have so often, some strange story, so that we may the better enjoy the morning before the hot sun heats up the day!' Do not fail in this, for our lives depend upon it!"

So the next morning, an hour before the dawn, just as Shahrazad had asked, Dunyazad came in with cups of cooled sherbet. She said to Shahrazad:

"Oh my dear sister! Do as you have so often done! Tell some strange story to lengthen the morning hour before the daylight reddens the sky."

"Most certainly, if this noble King allows me?"

The King, being restless, agreed. Shahrazad began to tell "The Story of the Merchant and the Genie."

This was a strange tale about a merchant who sat to rest under a tree to eat a piece of bread and a date. When he had eaten, the merchant threw away the date stone. Now in throwing it away he ought to have called out 'By your leave'.

Because he was alone, he did not. He just threw away the stone. No sooner had he done this than there appeared before him a huge Genie, with a sword in his hand. The Genie accused him of having just killed his son by hitting him on the chest with the date stone.

The merchant wept bitterly and begged the Genie to spare his life. "God be my witness," said the frightened merchant, "I meant no harm, it was only a date stone! I am not ready to die! I have a wife and children that I love. And I have not yet paid my debts nor set my affairs in order!"

But the Genie only answered that he must die. So at last the merchant asked the Genie to spare him for a year, so that he could appoint guardians for his children and pay his debts. He promised to come back on that very same day next year to the very spot and the Genie could do as he liked with him. The Genie agreed. And the merchant went sadly home; set his affairs in order; told his wife and children what had happened. When finished, the merchant said farewell to his weeping household and went back to the garden to keep his promise to the Genie.

At this point in the story Shahrazad stopped, saying with a sigh that there was no time for more because the sun had risen.

"But what happened to this unfortunate merchant?" asked her sister.

"Ah!" said Shahrazad. "The things that happened were very strange! Indeed this is nothing compared to the next part of the tale. I would gladly tell you if I had the time."

"By God," said the King, "I, too, should like to know whether the Genie did indeed kill the merchant."

"If the King spares me from the headsman," Shahrazad replied, "Tomorrow I will tell the end of this tale."

So the King got up, and went as usual to sit in judgment on his throne in the great court of the palace.

Now all that night the Grand Vizier had been mourning in his lonely house. He was too sad to eat or sleep. The next morning, when he came to present himself to the King, he had brought grave-clothes for his daughter. The King said nothing about Shahrazad, but went about his kingly duties without telling the Vizier what had happened to Shahrazad. However, since he had not been given the body of his daughter, the old man went home with hope that she was still alive.

An hour before dawn the next morning, Shahrazad's younger sister once more brought in cups of sherbet cooled with snow. Once more, she begged her sister to go on with the story of The Merchant and the Genie.

Shahrazad asked the King's permission. When it was granted, she continued. She explained that the merchant sat sadly in the garden, waiting for the Genie. As he sat he was joined by a handsomely dressed man who led a gazelle by a golden cord. And then a second man came up leading two black hounds on chains of silver. They both sat down to rest and asked the merchant why he sat alone in the garden and why he looked so sad. No sooner had he finished telling them what had happened, than the Genie appeared. He was as intimidating as ever with his sword in hand. The two strangers now begged the Genie not to be in such a hurry. And they began to explain why the wife of the one had been turned into a gazelle and the two brothers of the other had been turned into black dogs. They bargained with the Genie. If the Genie liked the stories and thought them strange enough, each would ask as his only reward half the life of the merchant! When he had listened to the stories, the Genie was so astonished that he was quite ready to agree to spare the merchant's life.

When she had got as far as this Shahrazad again stopped.

She said, "The sun has nearly risen! I wish that there were time to tell you also the story of The Fisherman and the Brass Bottle, for it is really much better and more wonderful than this tale of the Genie and the Merchant."

Exclaimed the King, "If it is an even better tale, I must certainly hear it! You may begin it at the same hour tomorrow!"

Once more all happened as before. The King went out to his day's work. Once more he said nothing about Shahrazad to the Grand Vizier.

However, Shahrazad managed to send word to her father telling him that she was alive and believed that her plan was going to succeed.

As was said before, Shahrazad knew and remembered a thousand tales. And she was particularly cunning in her way of telling them. Sometimes she would tell them so that one adventure was tangled in another, so that the King could not be sure of hearing what happened in one story unless he first listened to several other shorter tales. At other times her plan was to tell her stories in such a way that, at dawn, she would have to break off at some particularly exciting place. Each time she did this the King could not rest until he knew what happened next.

And so for a thousand nights, Shahrazad told her tales. But on the thousand and first night, the Queen did something that she had never done before. She finished one of her stories just as the sun rose, without leaving herself time to begin another. At this her young sister, Dunyazad, who had come as usual to listen, was amazed and alarmed. Seeing, however, that her sister was looking at the King with a smiling face, she said nothing, although it had always been her task to ask questions and to beg for yet another story.

"For a thousand nights, Oh King," Shahrazad said after a short silence, "I have enchanted the hour before the dawn with some tale of adventure or pleasure, ransacking the treasures of the Arabs, the Jews and the Persians and of the men of many other lands for your amusement. Have I, in all this time found favor in the eyes of the King? Can I now ask for a reward?"

"Oh most beloved of Queens, I have long known that you are the most excellent of women, the best of wives, and the light of my eyes! I have recovered from my bitterness towards women and all by reason of your excellence! How can I reward you?"

But his Queen answered him in a gentle voice, saying that she wanted no reward except that he would assure her father, so that he might know that she and the king's unborn son were in no danger.

So that morning with joy and gladness, the King bestowed honors on his old, faithful Grand Vizier. Queen Shahrazad and King Shahriyar lived a long and happy life.

Queen Shahrazad's power over the King did not come from superior force. It came from access to information. She was able to influence the King using information, where threats to his physical well-being would not have been effective. He felt secure in his power and was willing to be influenced by his wise Queen. She exercised a different but very effective form of power to influence her King.

A Look at the Emerging Basis for Power

Let's think about power in its broadest context. Power is not only the ability to take a life or to impose your will on another. Power is also the ability to understand and assimilate the information around us; to connect with the people around us and to cause things to happen in a constructive or destructive manner. Today, futurists tell us that there is a need to understand the changing basis for power. They tell us that the basis for power is evolving as technology changes our global society. They suggest that access to information is becoming more powerful than manufacturing capability, military might or financial wealth. Power, as we currently define it, is not only the ability to cause change; but it is also the ability to control yourself or others; or the ability to make things happen the way we choose. Technology is forcing us to reexamine this definition.

If money, manufacturing capability and military might become less strong and access to information replaces them, how does this change affect our lives and our values? How does it change the way we see the world? How does it force us to value other people of other cultures who have information we need? There are some who suggest that we still don't understand the concept of access to information. We are operating in the western world. In our world, control of intellectual property is important. We patent inventions and copyright books, movies, music, trademarks and slogans. Information of all kinds is controlled in the western world.

In Asia there has been a different view of knowledge. Many Asians say that there is an accessible body of knowledge which belongs to all of us. By these standards, the fact that I wrote the book that you are reading doesn't mean that I own the information in it. One can not own knowledge. One cannot control information. Think about this Asian attitude toward information in the context of the idea that access to information is becoming the new basis for power. We westerners have a view of access to information that is different from a large number of people with whom we expect to be able to conduct commerce and live in peace.

Changes in Personal Attitude

There are also personal attitude changes. Think about the way you live your individual lives. When I was a child, it was not considered child abuse for my father to spank me for doing something wrong. In fact, not punishing me was considered child abuse. Now there are laws to prohibit corporal punishment of children by teachers or parents. When I was a young professional coming into the workplace, I was expected to walk, talk, look (to the best of my ability) and think like the people right above me. I was expected to defer to their wisdom, experience and authority. If you have hired any young college graduates today, you know they have different attitudes.

Think about how you feel when somebody uses power and authority to bend you to their will. Thirty-five years ago using power and authority to control others was accepted and expected-- not so today. Changes in technological platforms, attitudes, and philosophies have changed our lives.

As this brave new world unfolds before you, new challenges come with it. You must learn to adapt to more people and more diversity than ever before. You must learn to communicate with more people who are different from yourself. To learn how to communicate with them, you must look within yourself.

Think about your feelings when being confronted with foreign attitudes, customs, practices or beliefs. Are you threatened by them or do they arouse your curiosity? When you are required to accommodate these differences, are you more willing to cooperate with others when you feel threatened or when you feel secure? Which makes you easier to influence on a permanent basis? It is my thesis that this world now requires skills of persuasion. Others cannot be forced to act or think in a desired way.

I want you to think now about the future. The world is facing two alternative futures: world destruction or global tolerance and peace. If world leaders continue to focus on power to dominate and kill, the world will pursue, global holocaust and destruction. If you are a movie fan as I am, you've seen *Mad Max* and *The Terminator* and many other doomsday movies. The basic thesis of these films is that the world will end in a nuclear holocaust and few people will be left. The survivors will revert to the culture, values and actions of cave people, a culture of violence, competition and desire for control over others.

The Father in the story, *Father and Son at the Hospital*, (Chapter Four, Step Three) had to employ doomsday-like tactics to save his son's life. The father had to raise the level of risk for the physicians and nurses before the hospital and medical staff would properly address a problem that they had caused. When their lives were at risk as well as the life of the son, they found a solution to the medical problems.

Many of us think about our own lives that way. We think about raising the level of risk. We think about confrontation. We think about the issues at stake. We think about negotiating. We talk about "win-win". But we really don't mean it. We mean, "I win". It may be "I win" for the community. It may be "I win" for the church. It may be "I win" for my family. It may be "I win" for my job. It takes effort to get past "I win". But in the coming technological age, cooperation will be more valuable than competition. We will be required to think "win-win" more often. It may eventually be a necessary mental habit for leadership survival.

Many current leaders' skills and attitudes may be as deficient as was Moses' in the following story. At the time of this story, Moses was an officer in the Egyptian army and was widely regarded as a master tactician. He was preparing himself to become the wise leader his people needed to take them out of Egypt into their promised land.

Moses Travels in Search of Knowledge

Moses and his close companion, servant and mentor went in search of wisdom. After some time, they found a wise man sitting on a rock.

He was a teacher, whom God had granted mercy and taught knowledge.

Moses said to him, "May I follow you and learn some of the good you have been taught?"

The teacher said, "You will not have patience with me. You do not know enough."

Moses said, "If God wills, you will find me patient. I will not disobey you."

The teacher said, "If you follow me, do not question what I do."

So they set out. When they got in a boat, the teacher made a hole in it. Moses said, "Have you made a hole in this boat to drown this poor family? You have surely done a bad thing."

The teacher said, "Did I not say you could not have patience with me?"

Moses replied, "I am sorry. Don't be too hard on me for asking."

They went on and met a boy. The teacher killed him. Moses said, "Have you slain an innocent person? You have indeed done a horrible thing."

The teacher said, "Did I not say you could not have patience with me?"

Moses replied, "If I ask you about anything after this, you can send me away."

So they went on until they came to a town. They asked the people for food. But the townspeople refused to feed Moses and the teacher. On the way out of the town they found a wall which was falling down. The teacher repaired it.

Moses said, "If you had wished, you could have taken payment for your work."

The teacher said, "This is the parting between you and me. Now I will inform you of the significance of my actions.

As for the boat, it belonged to poor people working on the river. I intended to damage it, for there was behind them a king who seized every boat by force. Once the king passed, the family could easily repair the small hole and the boat will be as good as new.

And for the boy, his parents were believers. God feared the boy would involve his parents in wrongdoing and disbelief. I killed him so that their Creator might give them a son better in purity and nearer to mercy, in his place.

As for the wall, it belonged to two orphaned boys in the city. There was a treasure beneath it which was their inheritance. Their father had been a righteous man. So God intended that they should attain their maturity and take out their treasure. I did not do it of my own accord. This is the significance of that with which you could not have patience."

This story moves me. I know that some people are bothered by the child being killed. Put that aside for a minute and think about the experience between the teacher and Moses, who as an army officer in Egypt was an established leader. No matter how well our leadership skills are developed; no matter how strong and wise people around us think we are; there is always room for growth.

President Lyndon Johnson made this point during the Viet Nam War when he was harassed by a young reporter who challenged him saying, "Mr. President, isn't it hard to do what's right?" President Johnson replied, "No son, it is not at all hard to do what's right. But it is hard to know what's right." This is something to think about. One alternate future ends in destruction because world leadership has steadfastly held on to its concept of power as the ability to kill or control others: "might over right; he who has the gold controls the rules."

As a youngster studying European history, I wondered why kings would arrange marriages between royal cousins, but other families feared creating deformed offspring and prohibited inbreeding. Someone explained that the kings' fears of losing power was stronger than their knowledge of biological sciences. Inbreeding eventually put deformed incompetents on European thrones.

Today we face a similar challenge. Corporate boards are looking for creative talent capable of seeing issues differently and making substantive changes in attitudes. However, most boards have continued mental inbreeding, hiring one CEO after another with the same educational, cultural and experiential background. They have not yet attempted to reach outside of their own communities to find capable people with differing cultural and educational backgrounds.

Within the past year, chief executives have been hired at IBM, Hughes Aircraft, General Motors, Lehman, NBC News and other major corporations. However, much of corporate America is changing the guard by playing "musical chairs". Almost like the children's game, these men are going around to the music as each turn brings another merger or bankruptcy, therefore fewer chairs. Few new corporate executives have entered top management; CEOs are jumping from one company to another under the pretense of being outsiders and therefore masters of change.

An exception is George C. Wolfe, the new producer of the New York Shakespeare Festival. When founder Joseph Papp's hand picked successor, JoAnn Akalaitis, was ousted by the Board in favor of Wolfe, an agent of creative change was sought. Wolfe brings an African American sensitivity, vision and perspective which will give the New York Shakespeare Festival a fresh viewpoint and brighter future. JoAnn Akalaitis was more of the same, old ideas in a new more competitive world. Although Akalaitis charges gender discrimination in her early ouster from the helm, it is really an indication that board leadership in corporate America is beginning to understand that stewardship in the next generation will require executive leadership with the fortitude to exact change. Boards are responding to real risks of being held accountable for their company losing its competitive advantages in this new global environment where the rules, values and outcomes are no longer controlled by Europe and North America.

Hughes Aircraft's CEO, C. Michael Armstrong seems to be another exception. While head of IBM's global operations, he realized that it was time "to do something new" with his life. To sell effectively in very different cultures, Armstrong must have learned cultural flexibility. He says as much in describing his first goal at Hughes Aircraft which is to earn the respect of top management and make that a mutual respect. He seems to understand that mutual respect is important. Cultural flexibility emphasizes the need for mutual respect as the basis for effective communication.

The world's economic future depends upon corporate leadership realizing that their efforts are redundant as long as they continue to hire CEOs from similar environments. This is mental inbreeding similar to the European royal inbreeding which produced imbecile kings and eventually undermined the effectiveness of many European nations. With continued mental inbreeding, corporate jobs, security, power and prestige will further erode.

As we consider the future of our world, there is another choice. This alternative is best illustrated by the story of the two brothers who inherited a farm and worked the field together (Chapter Four, Step Seven). At harvest time each brother, concerned about the financial needs of the other, secreted a substantial portion of his share into the other's barn. Because they both did this, neither lost from his generosity. In strong partnerships where the partners understand that their interests are interdependent, they do not lose by looking out for their partner's well-being in addition to their own. We can learn to do this by habit. We can use cultural flexibility to open attitudes. This will build a world where many of its inhabitants use the principles employed by these two brothers and act in their "enlightened self interest" as these brothers have done.

We can find ways to build connections between ourselves and other people in such a way that we can respect, admire, trust and care for people other than ourselves. The epitome of this is cultural flexibility, the skill which allows us to act in the best interest of people who are very different from ourselves.

People celebrate diversity in the United States. In international circles people are learning to celebrate diversity also. But it is not effective only to celebrate diversity. Diversity by itself is divisive. People must learn to celebrate diversity within the context of the human family with the understanding that there is something to be admired, cherished and respected in each person.

From this beginning we should use differences to build a rich organization, community, company, friendship, family or world. Cultural flexibility can become the basis for an alternate future that is not merely a couple of brothers sharing a crop, but nations of the world sharing their intellectual and physical resources; sharing their responsibility for maintaining and improving the environment and sharing their responsibility for caring for each other in important and meaningful ways.

CHAPTER VII

Connecting South Africa's Rainbow People

Introduction

The New South Africa is an example of the way to begin to practice cultural flexibility. The relationship between South African people is becoming similar to the relationship between the brothers who inherited the farm. South Africa is not just an important economy in the region of Southern Africa but it is an important human example for the rest of the world.

South Africa is in transition from one kind of leadership to another, from one set of values to another. The world is watching to see if South Africa becomes a family that works together, showing us a way to celebrate humanity and diversity in a culturally flexible manner. It is fertile ground for growing the new attitudes of tolerance and respect which has been fostered by forgiveness extended to their former oppressors by President Mandela and his Rainbow People.

President Nelson M. Mandela

"Those who remark on my tight schedule do not understand the good feeling I have each evening when I know I have had a productive day," declares South African President Nelson Mandela. He is explaining his ability to thrive on such a hectic pace even though he is a seventy-six year old man who has spent twenty-seven years of his life confined in jail. His face glows with delight at the end of another twelve hour day as he talks about the energy he gets from his daily sense of accomplishment for his beloved country.

In person, Mandela's quiet power suggests an inner peace and comfort with a personal mission much larger than himself. As he reflects on the early years of his difficult struggle, he seems to be reconnecting with a personal hero through the presence of a good friend.

"Paul Robeson was a great artist and a great friend of the African National Congress (ANC) long before it was a popular cause. Harry Belafonte, my friend has continued in the Robeson tradition, championing the causes of under-privileged people of the world," President Mandela says with a smile. Citing an incident when Paul Robeson, denied a passport by the U.S. government, kept a London performance date by performing via telephone, Mandela glowed with pride and admiration. To Mandela this demonstrated Robeson's power and determination in the face of strong opposition. It inspired him to live like his role model. He said that he treasures the memory of Robeson. He was pleased that his friend, actor and singer Harry Belafonte, has reminded him of the strength of Robeson, the artist.

But President Mandela is not without problems. When he explains the economic issues facing his presidency, he does so with compassion, almost pleading. He talks about 50% unemployment, people cooking with water infested by tadpoles and other unknowable vermin. They have no running water, no electricity and share small cramped shacks with multiple generations. He pleads for help in providing good food, clothing, shelter and health care for the thirty million under-privileged majority of South Africa.

"We have people capable of solving our problems," he insists, "What we need is resources. We need investment especially from the United States, which is the world's leading champion for democracy." He said that South Africa must look to the United

States to help their fragile democracy by encouraging reinvestment in South Africa. Their people will not wait patiently for gradual improvement of their lives. They want visible signs of improvement soon. These visible signs of improvement cannot be created without outside help.

"We have a government of unity where people have put aside the hatred and fears of their past and are learning to work together." He illustrates this by listing the cabinet seats held by each major party. "In our government Inkatha has three cabinet ministers; the National Party has six cabinet ministers." He says they are serving side by side with the ANC's eighteen ministers.

An Invitation to North America

"Millions of jobs have to be created. Hundreds of thousands of houses have to be built and electrified. Both the young and old have to be educated and their health cared for. More food must be produced." These goals are enumerated by Thabo Mbeki, Executive Deputy President, as he acknowledges the awesome challenges facing President Nelson Mandela and the new South African government. He continues to explain to the spellbound audience of U.S. and South African business leaders assembled in Atlanta, that these challenges mean business for U.S. companies. He and other government officials who spoke during this two day conference talked about "Investing in People". They want Americans to realize that this investment in the people of South Africa would bring business to U.S. companies.

There is an open invitation to U.S. businesses from the Mandela Administration and South African business leaders. They have expressed an interest in working with African Americans where possible. The Mandela Administration seems to understand the importance of building black economic power in North

America as well as South Africa and are willing to use their new found political power to encourage progress here.

The Rainbow People, (as President Mandela calls them), representing business and the new South African government want foreign investment. They also want access to foreign technology, management and markets. Unlike many of the new republics in Eastern Europe, these South Africans present a clear plan for investing in people, which is designed to raise the standard of living for South Africans and thereby build a greater demand for products and services made by or in partnership with foreign companies. In the words of Bishop Desmond Tutu, "I was known as Mr. Sanctions. Now I want to be known as Mr. Investment!" He and others emphasize that "We are not coming with a begging bowl. We are inviting investment for a fair return and long term benefit to both investor and investment recipient."

This grand experiment began with the election of a non-racial government. Black economic empowerment is next. As Ms. Dawn Mokholo, Senior General Manager of the South Africa power company (ESKOM), explains, "We are building a nation where Robin Hood will have no work." This refers to the concept of social democracy endorsed by the new government. It is an expectation that people who have been able to earn substantial incomes will voluntarily give their excess to those in need. In the early days of the United States' Industrial Revolution examples of high-income people with a social conscience included Andrew Carnegie, the Rockefeller family, the Ford family and others who funded libraries, private foundations and other institutions for the public.

President Mandela's and Bishop Tutu's work is showing results. According to Reuters, the international wire service, "U.S. investment in South Africa has soared since September 1993, when Nelson Mandela called on the world to end economic sanctions against the country." It cites a survey which shows that thirty American companies have acquired subsidiaries or affiliates, opened branch offices, or placed employees in South Africa in the last year. The estimated total is now 169 U.S. firms in South Africa. Some returnees include Eastman Kodak, Honeywell, IBM, and Sara Lee.

In a unique move which should be studied and emulated by others, Pepsi returned with Black partners. PepsiCo established New Age Beverages, a $20 million investment joined by African Americans including Black Enterprise publisher, Earl Graves and actor Danny Glover. The team includes Black South Africans in both investment and management roles.

Changing Attitudes

The link between the thirty million African Americans and the thirty million Black South Africans is not as obvious today as it was when South Africa was struggling for political freedom. However the Reconstruction and Development Program (RDP), South Africa's hope for the under privileged, will only succeed if we strengthen this link. African Americans and Black South Africans must build alliances which will strengthen the economic opportunities for both groups. They must bring the rest of the developed world to the table with them.

"African Americans do not want to understand South Africa. They want to believe that our racial and cultural situation is the same as theirs here in the United States. We are not the same!" So says Imogen Mkhize, an impressive Zulu woman now a second year MBA student at Harvard Business School. "An example of what I mean is Sarafina, the movie starring Whoopi Goldberg, filmed in Soweto. This movie implies that our problem in the schools was the course material. But it was much deeper than that. We were being taught in Afrikaans, not English. White children were taught in English. This system isolated us from the rest of the world. No one speaks or writes in Afrikaans outside of South

Africa. We were learning useless material in a useless language. The system was designed to keep blacks in ignorance."

Attitudes of African Americans have changed dramatically since the election of President Nelson Mandela to form the first non-racial government in South Africa. Upon returning from my first trip, African American friends warned me not to admit that I had traveled to South Africa and not to tell anyone that I counted a white South African family as friends. Today those of us who were interested in the plight of this nation, torn apart by the evils of apartheid, are viewed in a much different light. We are held in much higher esteem than those who have later come to realize the opportunity and responsibility. South Africa presents an opportunity to connect with very capable people in commercial, political and religious endeavors and a responsibility to demonstrate respect for the accomplishments and capabilities of our brothers and sisters. South Africans have built a coalition which has risen above apartheid to form a non-racial government and a non-racial society which will stand as a model for the world to follow.

Many changes are being made in South Africa and other parts of the world today. As opportunities open, it is important to be prepared to participate. Travel and first hand observation is not available to all. However, those who can should see as much of the world as possible and bring back what they are learning for others who have not traveled. On each of my visits, South Africa has seemed to have become an entirely different country. The people have adapted to their new relationships with amazing speed.

Background

South Africa has 35 million people in 458 thousand square miles. For comparison, Southeastern United States has 52 million people in 471 thousand square miles. I have toured Black townships in South Africa during and after apartheid. There was not much improvement in the living conditions I saw although apartheid laws had been rescinded. The poverty in Black South African townships is unimaginable if you have not seen it first hand. However it is no more devastating than poverty in the Mississippi Delta or homelessness on the streets of Washington, DC.

There are two dominant groups of whites in South Africa, the Afrikaans and the English. Afrikaans generally hold civil service and politically elected government jobs. Other Afrikaans hold working class or middle management positions in business. The English generally hold top management positions in business. Few serve in government, in either elected or civil service positions. Therefore, Afrikaans see themselves as the people who will lose most from political and social integration with non-whites.

Social Interaction

At a Pizza Hut restaurant in Johannesburg, South Africa, I had an experience reflective of the past and present times in South Africa. Yes, Pizza Hut made it to South Africa!

While I was getting a salad from the self-serve salad bar, a young Afrikaans boy reached across the aisle to my table and took the salt shaker. He took it for use by himself and his audience, two young Afrikaans girls who were sitting at the table with him. I saw the act. He saw me watching him take the salt shaker. He demonstrated a belligerent attitude. He was looking for an altercation that would give him a chance to show off for the girls sitting with him.

There was a young Englishman about the same age as the Afrikaans boy sitting at the next table. Before I returned to my seat, the Englishman sitting next to my table reached through the lattice work and put his salt shaker onto my table. He was with a young woman about his age. Neither of them spoke of the incident, nor looked to me for acknowledgement of his action.

Later a woman about 35 joined the three Afrikaans across the aisle from me. She treated the Black man who was serving their table and mine, in a very derogatory manner. She insisted that he sell her a slice of pizza. He was obviously new on the job, very nervous and unsure of himself (until then Blacks had not been hired in such restaurants for serving positions; their work was limited to clean up). His instructions had been to sell pizzas complete and to send customers buying only a slice to the takeout window, near the entrance to the restaurant. After some discussion, his manager allowed him to sell the woman a slice of pizza. She gloated," I knew you could do it, boy!", to the approval of her young table companions.

The very next year, people in the same Pizza Hut restaurant were acting quite differently. White, Asian and Black Africans were eating without incident. The store manager was a well-poised young Black African man. This seemed to be an entirely different nation of people than the experience described above revealed.

Management and Technical Capabilities

People outside of South Africa have the mistaken notion that all or most of Black South Africa is illiterate, disenfranchised and untrainable. However, the women street vendors of Durban and the men I talked with in institutional offices show much potential.

Women entrepreneurs (street vendors) were spending five days per week selling handicrafts on the sidewalk. They sleep on side streets in Durban each night and return to their stalls each day. They are providing a livelihood for themselves and the crafts-people back home. People of similar and possibly less ambition and business acumen have succeeded in retail establishments of major North American cities. With proper preparation and training, some of these women can become effective salespeople and more.

Before the end of apartheid, men working in a local Durban institution believed that they were paid much lower than their non-Black counterparts. They are well trained artisans. One is fluent in several languages and has translated major texts into the Zulu language for use in educating his people. Their formal training in music and performing arts make them trainable for management positions in the new South Africa. They seem to be representative of a large under-utilized but well-trained cadre of professionals who were waiting for their turn at management and executive positions in government, business and educational institutions.

Lest we question the capability of Black business managers and professionals in the new South Africa, "Business Day", the South Africa national business newspaper, published a special report of the Black Management Forum (BMF). BMF, started in 1976 by one hundred managers in the Johannesburg area, represents over 1,500 members. It has identified a potential membership of more than 3,000. BMF represents people who are or aspire to be managers in the corporate world. They do not generally represent business owners or professionals such as accountants. However, they do maintain close ties with the Association of Black Accountants of South Africa (ABASA) and other organizations which represent the professions and skilled trades.

Jeff van Rooyen

Jeff van Rooyen, Director of the New South Africa Group at the international accounting firm, Deloitte & Touche, has suggested that ABASA can play a major role in economic empowerment. Accounting, the language of business, is a common foundation for any economy. He also believes that an important step is to begin to form strategic alliances across the Atlantic Ocean, between joint teams of Black owned businesses and major companies in the United States and South Africa. These strategic alliances must have specific targets for economic empowerment and career development for Black South Africans.

Jeff van Rooyen is a Black man and an executive in South Africa. He studied accountancy and served articles (required apprenticeship) with one of the major worldwide accounting firms. Seven years ago he left that firm to start a practice of his own. At the time, Black South Africans were not allowed to rent property or own businesses in the city. So Jeff began his practice in the nearby township. He served fledgling businesses in their communities and began to develop advisory roles with the major political parties. He advised the leaders of the African National Congress (ANC) and Inkatha on financial and economic issues of importance to the changing South Africa.

With the lifting of bans and apartheid laws, he could now maintain an accounting office in Johannesburg. His leadership in integrating the accounting profession put him in line to join the Public Accounting and Audit Board, the licensing and regulatory body for CAs in South Africa. He also joined similar leadership bodies of the South African Institute of Chartered Accountants (SAICA). Because of his growing recognition as an astute business and economic advisor he was invited to address an assembly of U.S. Senators and Congressmen at the Aspen Institute's program on economic empowerment in Bermuda. Then the major worldwide accountancy firm Deloitte & Touche invited him to join them as their first Black South African partner.

Although now in a position of enviable influence and financial stability, Jeff understands the pain of segregation and violence first hand. He lost a brother to apartheid induced violence several years ago. He takes heart and encouragement from his sense of personal mission and relies on guidance from scriptures.

One of his favorite Bible stories is the story of Jonah (Bible, Old Testament, Book of Jonah). He says that he often feels like Jonah as he struggles for economic empowerment in South Africa.

As he tells the story, "Jonah ran from God because he was afraid of the people's reaction to the message God wanted him to deliver. When he finally gave in and preached the message - telling the people to stop their evil ways and repent or be destroyed by God, the people repented and God did not destroy them. Then Jonah turned back to God in exasperation, "I knew this would happen. That is why I did not want to carry your message!".

Jonah was worried about his personal credibility and standing with his countrymen. The risks of leadership were initially too heavy for him to bear. Once he had accomplished his assigned mission, he was afraid that his countrymen would not appreciate what he had done for them.

Jeff said he often has similar misgivings about carrying messages of change and warning to white South Africa. Leadership is often thrust upon him. However, those asking him to lead often do not appreciate the personal risks he must take, nor do they appreciate what he has accomplished on their behalf. He is often like Jonah, a reluctant prophet/leader whose admonitions and warnings are followed so that the threats of dire consequences never are fulfilled. It is difficult for his countrymen to recognize or appreciate what he has done for them. He reluctantly takes one leadership position after another, for the benefit of his successors, his country and the world.

Sheik Ahmed Deedat

The image South Africa brings to mind is Black Africans and freedom from apartheid. The image of Sheik Ahmed Deedat, the president of the Islamic Propagation Center International (IPCI), brings to mind Islam, learned scholarship and Indian culture. The two came together nicely in Durban. South Africa and India are combined in the practice and life of Islam in a most comforting and pleasant way.

A day with the six-foot, seventy-six year old, white haired dynamo leaves a lasting impression. One minute he is relating the story of Onan and explaining why it was inserted into the Bible story of Joseph. An hour later, he is discussing economic policy and the value of Islamic banking with me, the U.S. trade advisor and the president of his Durban based bank. His mental and physical energy and versatility are inspiring.

Sheik Deedat is not without controversy in Islamic scholarship. Largely self-taught and an accomplished orator, he is sometimes put down by more traditional Islamic scholars for his lack of educational credentials and the controversy of his speeches. Deedat is more familiar with the Bible than many Christian ministers I have known. He is fond of comparing the Bible with the Quran suggesting that the Quran has held more closely to the original revelations from God than has the widely translated and many versioned Bible. He has held widely publicized debates with Christian personalities such as Jimmy Swaggert and others on this subject.

As South Africa reemerges in world leadership, the vision, versatility and energy of people like Sheik Deedat will shape its future.

Conclusion

"African Americans can help themselves and South Africans at the same time. We are not the same. But we can learn from each other," asserts Imogen Mkhize, the second year Harvard MBA student. Prior to study at Harvard, she was the Executive Director of the Association of Black Accountants of South Africa (ABASA). Between her first and second year she worked in strategic planning for Owens Corning Fiberglas, a major United States manufacturing company. She is one of a growing number of Black South Africans who have the education and experience to make a substantial difference in the economic future of South Africa and the world.

Many well-trained African American professionals and managers are reaching a "glass ceiling", which impedes further progress for them within the United States. Some African American owned businesses are reaching for saturated markets in North America. Now is the time to join forces between major and African American owned U.S. businesses to expand vehicles for reinvestment, technology and management transfer to potential business partners in South Africa. Now is the time for major U.S. businesses to look for international leadership and understanding from their well trained African American managers and executives. Doing both will stimulate national and global economies and ease the unrest which will continue as erosion of United States affirmative action and procurement preferences increases.

The New South Africa is an example to the world. African Americans are an untapped resource for the world. Combining these two forces will bring greater opportunity and deeper understanding of people throughout the world.

Epilogue

Technology has changed the world, forcing people to interact with people of other races, cultures, religions and customs on a much more frequent basis than in the Industrial Age. This interaction builds the need for members of each society to learn to coexist and thrive within a multi-cultural or culturally diverse workplace, classroom or community. Developing the mental habit of cultural flexibility will make this forced coexistence more manageable and possibly even pleasant for many previously hostile and rigid individuals.

Technology has produced an information overload which is tempting leaders of all types - executives, managers, politicians and clergy - to abandon "gut feelings" in favor of exhaustive analysis for decision-making. Experienced executives value the mental habit of intuitive thinking, but are having difficulty in transferring this respect for intuition to their younger executives. Use of folklore and stories can help the process of developing and honing intuitive thinking for emerging executives and leaders.

All people of whatever nation or culture are capable of expressing joy and sorrow, hope and despair, acceptance and rejection, submission or aggressiveness, logical and illogical thoughts, and a whole range of other feelings and thinking. The vigor, style, and manner in which these thought processes or emotional feelings are expressed are conditioned by the culture in which the individual was nurtured. It is said frequently that people behave the same the world over. True, but despite the similarities in the foundations of culture there are also significant differences in behavior based on the degree of assimilation of the mores, folkways, and taboos both of the dominant and sub-cultural groups.

This book is a contribution to the development of the two necessary mental habits needed for effective leadership in the future, namely cultural flexibility and intuitive thinking. My thoughts about these concepts are best embodied in the following closing story.

In Your Hands

There is a story told of a wise man who lived on a hill, outside of the city. He was reported to be the wisest man in the area. People went to him for advice. He was wise in the advice.

As it seems to always happen in the city, there were some teenage boys who felt that they were wiser than the old man. They decided to trap him. The boys caught a baby robin and plotted together to fool the old man. They would put the bird in their hands and go to find the old man. When they found him, they would ask him, "Old man, what do we have in our hands?"

Of course, the old man would reply, "A bird," being able to see its feathers. Their next question would be, "Is it alive or dead?" If the old man said, "alive," they planned to crush the bird in their hands and kill it. If the old man said the bird was "dead", they would let it loose to fly away.

Having plotted their scheme the boys went to the hill in search of the old man. They confronted him, "Old man, what do we have in our hands?"

"A bird," the wise man answered.

"Old man, is the bird alive or dead?" challenged the boys.

The old man looked all three boys in the eye at the same time, as only a wise old man could do.

And he responded, "It is in your hands, my sons."

The future of our lives, the future of our nation, the future of the world, the choice of the alternate futures, peace or destruction, is in our hands. I ask you to join with me to pass the message about our alternative futures. There are 5.5 billion people in the world today. I cannot reach all of them. So we must share the responsibility. Please pass along this message and these folktales as far and wide as possible.

Appendices

This appendix provides additional information and opportunities for expanding your personal growth.

Glossary

Definitions: The Cultural Cousins

Cultural Flexibility is the mental habit of overlooking superficial differences of physical appearance, personal beliefs, dietary preferences and life style to find a basis for mutual respect and communication.

Cultural Arrogance is the mental habit of allowing obsession with superficial differences of others to destroy communication.

Cultural Diversity describes an environment in which people of differing backgrounds teach, learn, live, work, worship or communicate and otherwise communicate with each other.

Cultural Sensitivity is the ability to understand and empathize with a person or a group of people whose demonstrated values, way of life, religion, conventions and possibly language are different from your own.

Intuitive Thought is the mental habit of combining intellect and emotion to reach beyond the scope of either.

Stories Index

Cultural Flexibility Reading List

For an Understanding of the Changing Environment

1. *Third Wave* by Alvin Toffler (Bantam, New York, 1984).

2. *Megatrends* by John Naisbett (Warner Books, New York, 1988).

3. *Age of Unreason* by Charles Handy (Harvard Business School Press, Boston, 1991).

These books give varying viewpoints and perspectives on the economic and social trends of the recent past and predictable future. Although some of the authors have published books subsequent to the ones listed here, these are recommended for gaining a basic understanding of the thought process involved in predicting structural changes in the global environment. They analyze our social, economic and political environment in understandable and useable fashion.

For a Foundation to Build the Skill of Cultural Flexibility

1. *The Art of Getting Your Own Sweet Way* by Phil Crosby (McGraw-Hill, New York, 1972).

2. *The Greatest Salesman in the World* by Og Mandino (Bonanza Books, New York, 1968).

3. *How to Win Friends and Influence People* by Dale Carnegie and Dorothy Carnegie (S&S Trade, New York, 1981).

4. *Winning by Intimidation* by Robert Ringer (Los Angeles Nook Publishers, Los Angeles, 1974).

5. *Think and Grow Rich* by Napoleon Hill (Napoleon Hill Foundation and Wilshire Book Company, Hollywood, CA 1986) or *Think and Grow Rich an African American Choice* by Napoleon Hill and Dennis Kimbrow (Fawcett Columbine Book, New York, 1991).

These books emphasize personal development but each shows ways to become more effective by developing the ability to listen to and understand others.

To Begin the Process of Learning Respect for Other Cultures

1. Any version of the Bible currently unfamiliar to you.

2. The Quran (Muslim Scripture); Teachings of Confucius, Teachings of Buddha and other similar religious theologies.

3. Folktales and myths from other nations. Many public libraries have a section on mythologies of other cultures.

You may be surprised by the familiar themes in stories from cultures and countries that are very different from the United States, democracy and Christianity. It should be an interesting and entertaining experience for any who decide to explore.

Stories and Folklore Reading List

Although many of my most treasured stories come from people who have folktales handed down from prior generations, there are several books I have used in collecting stories for speeches and concerts. They include:

Talk That Talk edited by Linda Goss and Marian E. Barnes (Simon and Schuster/Touchstone, New York, 1989).

Moses Man of the Mountain by Zora Neale Hurston (University of Illinois Press, Chicago, 1984).

Mules and Men by Zora Neale Hurston (Indiana University Press, Bloomington, 1978).

The Best of South African Short Stories (Readers Digest Association of South Africa, Cape Town, 1991).

The Exploits of the Incomparable Mullah Nasrudin by Idries Shah (The Octagon Press, London, 1966).

Kalila and Dimna, Selected Fables of Bidpai retold by Ramsay Wood (AA Knopf, Inc. distributed by Random House, New York, 1980).

African Folktales by Roger D. Abrahams (Pantheon Books a division of Random House, New York, 1983).

Best Loved Folktales of the World by Joanna Cole (Anchor Press Doubleday, New York, 1982).

Fellowship Opportunities to Ease Career Trauma and Develop Cultural Sensitivity

Many major U.S. businesses are eliminating middle management jobs by the thousands. The U.S. Department of Labor reports more than 1.5 million professionals and managers out of work, who will remain unemployed over one year. On the other hand, NAFTA and GATT, new democracies in Eastern Europe and South Africa, are opening new career opportunities for United States professionals and managers. The German offices of major and smaller firms have been stretched to the maximum since the reunification of Germany. East European nations are clamoring for accounting services and business training. Mexican and Latin American businesses are in great need of technical environmental engineering and management training in making the transition into the new North American Free Trade Area. Many businesses in China and Southeast Asia need business training and western management know-how as they penetrate new markets in Japan and the Americas. South African businesses need upgraded business systems, training and North American partners for the new African American owned businesses and institutions now entering the market.

International Fellowships

For those interested in broadening their career or business horizons, now is a good time to consider some of the many educational and experiential programs available. Recognize that Cultural Flexibility is now needed in addition to specific training in professional or technical skills. The fellowship experience combines education and experience for professionals and managers with proven leadership talent. Following are descriptions of six such programs.

U.S. - Japan Leadership Program
Sponsored by the Japan Society

Annual fellowships are being offered for the U.S. - Japan Leadership Program, sponsored by the Japan Society, Inc. This fellowship seeks U.S. citizens in their thirties and early forties with demonstrated leadership and career achievements. Candidates may come from journalism, business, education, government and labor.

This is a guided self-education program requiring residence in Japan and continued involvement in U.S. - Japan relations. Fellows will prepare for Japan residency by reading, studying the Japanese language and participating in conferences (including a two-day orientation for all active fellows). Residency in Japan is expected to be for a minimum of two (2) months during the fellowship year.

Each fellow will have a prominent Japanese institution as a co-host during the residency and a wide range of Japanese resources will be introduced. The fellowship will provide basic business and living expenses for the Japan residency.

For further information:
Connie Marshall, Program Officer or
Ms. Ruri Kawashima, Director
U.S. - Japan Program, Japan Society
333 E 47th St
New York, NY 10017
212-832-1155; fax 755-6752

Eisenhower Exchange Fellowship

The Eisenhower Exchange Fellowship is for men and women aged between twenty-eight and forty-five. The USA program is for U.S. citizens who have demonstrated outstanding achievement in a professional field. Countries available for residency and study are Argentina, Greece, New Zealand, Taiwan and Turkey.

Fellows will receive four weeks of closely scheduled professional consultations, visits, and conferences throughout the assigned country. Schedules are tailored to individual objectives and availability. The fellowship year begins in October of each year.

For further information:
Diane M. Shoemaker, Program Officer
Eisenhower Exchange Fellowships Inc
256 South 16th St
Philadelphia, PA 19102
215-546-1738; fax 546-4567; telex 902028 GLOBAL, INC

White House Fellowship
Sponsored by the Commission on White House Fellowships

Although White House Fellowships are not all internationally oriented, there are appointments to the Department of Commerce, the Office of the U.S. Trade Representative, the State Department and others which provide international experience and perspective.

The White House Fellowships are a dual experience combining a meaningful work assignment with a rigorous education program. Although the year long work assignment is not intended to fit into a fellow's previous specialty, it aims to use each fellow's abilities and to develop the fellow's skills in the broadest sense possible. In working with senior federal government executives, the work assignment puts fellows into the policy making process and provides executive level experience with the process of running the U.S. Federal Government.

Fellows also participate in an education program which includes a series of off-the-record meetings with top-level government and private sector leaders, including former U.S. presidents. Over the years fellows have traveled throughout the world examining international issues and U.S. foreign policy from centers of power offering diverse perspectives.

Applicants for White House Fellowships are expected to be experienced leaders in education, religion, business, social services, the professions and community service who are under forty years of age. Fellows are paid a federal government salary commensurate with their qualifications and responsibilities for the full year of the program. Selection of White House Fellows is made on a nonpartisan basis. If you are interested in learning more about the White House Fellowships write:

The President's Commission of White House Fellowships
712 Jackson Place NW
Washington, DC 20503
Tel 202-395-4522; fax 202-395-6179

Japan Exchange and Teaching Program

The Japan Exchange and Teaching Program promotes mutual understanding between Japan and Australia, Canada, France, Germany and the United States. It offers young college graduates of the target nations the opportunity to work in Japanese local governments, public and private schools. The program operates on an annual basis. In 1991 JETP sponsored 2,874 participants from eight countries.

Candidates may apply for one of two types of positions - Coordinator for International Relations or Assistant English Teacher. Contracts are for one year commencing in July of each year.

Eligible candidates must be under thirty-five years of age, hold at least a bachelor's degree, have working knowledge of the English language and have an interest in Japan.

For further information contact:
Paige Cottingham, Coordinator-US-Japan Project
Joint Center for Political Studies
1090 Vermont NW, Ste 1100
Washington, DC 20005-4961
202-789-3500; fax 789-6388

U.S. Peace Corps

The Peace Corps recruits volunteers for work in all parts of the developing world. Today six thousand volunteers in over seventy countries in the Caribbean, South America, Central America, Africa, Asia, the Pacific and Central Europe. Specific programs have been designed to make the best use of people with business education and skills. In their two year appointment, volunteers are exposed to a wide range of experiences: from serving as bookkeeper for local businesses to advising high ranking government officials. These experiences vary daily.

Eligible candidates must be at least eighteen years old. Married couples are welcome if both will be volunteers. Most assignments require a college degree or three to five years work experience.

An assignment can be as close as Barbados or Jamaica or as far away as Western Samoa in the Pacific. Many former volunteers have developed rewarding careers in international business, education or government. Their Peace Corps experience gave them a head start in their careers.

In some parts of the country the Peace Corps holds periodic briefings for potential volunteers. The Washington Area Office holds monthly information sessions where former volunteers answer questions, a recruiter explains the application process and a short video shows actual Peace Corps experiences.

For further information contact:
Peace Corps, Box 941
Public Response, 9th Floor
1990 K Street NW
Washington, DC 20526
202-606-3000 ext 941

Council on Foreign Relations

This program is designed to encourage cooperation between scholarship and stewardship in international affairs. The Council offers a number of grants to candidates between the ages of twenty-seven and thirty-five from government, academia, business and the professions. Successful candidates will be (1) promising people in public service who have displayed notable intellectual gifts and whose professional growth would benefit from a period of reflection and writing about important contemporary issues in international relations; and (2) those now in private life whose professional development and potential contributions to foreign policy would particularly benefit from a period of active public service. Nominations are expected before September 15 of each year.

For further information:
Kempton Dunn, Director, Membership & Fellowship Affairs
Council on Foreign Relations
58 East 68th St.
New York, NY 10021
212-734-0400; fax 861-2701

World Trading Blocks

G-7 (Group of 7): United States of America, United Kingdom, Canada, Japan, Germany, Italy, France. Russia has been admitted to this group as a discussant on security issues.

EU (European Union): England, France, Italy, Spain, Germany, Greece, Portugal, Denmark, Luxembourg, Belgium, Ireland, Holland.

EFTA (European Free Trade Association): Austria, Liechtenstein, Iceland, Finland, Norway, Sweden, Switzerland.

EEA (European Economic Area): European Community and European Free Trade Association.

NAFTA (North American Free Trade Area): Canada, United States of America and Mexico.

CIS (Commonwealth of Independent States): Russia, Kazakhstan, Kyrgyzstan, Tajikistan, Turkmenistan, Uzbekistan, Azerbaijan, Armenia, Ukraine, Moldova, Belarus.

ASEAN (Association of South East Asian Nations): The Philippines, Thailand, Malaysia, Singapore, Indonesia and Brunei.

EAEG (East Asian Economic Group): ASEAN, Japan, China, South Korea, Hong Kong, Taiwan and Viet Nam.

Southern Africa: Namibia, Botswana, Zimbabwe, Lesotho, Mozambique, South Africa.

Caricom: Antigua and Barbuda, the Bahamas, Barbados, Dominica, Grenada, Jamaica, Montserrat, Saint Christopher and Nevis, Saint Lucia, Saint Vincent and the Grenadines, Trinidad and Tobago, Belize and Guyana.

Central American Market: Guatemala, El Salvador, Honduras, Costa Rica and Nicaragua.

Andean Pact: Venezuela, Colombia, Ecuador, Peru and Bolivia.

G-3 (Group of 3): Colombia, Venezuela and Mexico.

Mercosur (Southern Cone Zone): Brazil, Paraguay, Argentina and Uruguay.

Index

Order Information

Stories and Folktales on Audio Cassette
Retold by Tom Watson:

Stories of the World-Volume 1: Africa and Beyond

Mullah Nasrudin Introduction (From Persia).

"Gold Coins" - Money lender's joke on Nasrudin backfires.

"Keep a Secret" - Local gossip wants to pass on a secret.

"Truth" - a king wants to force everyone to tell truth.

Sadaquat (West African folktale) - Seven princes travel the world one after another. They each encounter a magical island with fruit trees that grow instantaneously from discarded seeds. Sadaquat, the youngest of these sons is the last one to travel.

Stories of the World - Volume 2: You Need Oranges

You Need Oranges (Modified from Middle East folktale) - Impatient medical apprentice learns the value of giving time/attention as well as medical care.

Little League (United States) - Young boy's new motivation after father's death.

Gideon (from Bible) - Reluctant leader finds trust in God and routs enemy.

Mullah Nasrudin Introduction (From Middle East and India)

"Fussy Scholar" - Nasrudin's passenger, chiding him about his grammar, learns practical side of life.

"Joseph and the Robe" - Nasrudin's friend, Joseph, accompanies him on a round of visits wearing his new robe.

"Whose Shot Was That?" - Nasrudin's students ask him to participate in local fair. He illustrates attitudes and results with his shots.

Stories of the World - Volume 3: Wisdom of Willie

Willie Introduction (Character Modified from Middle East and Indian Tales.

"Saved His Life" - Willie shows irony of misguided religious fervor.

"Caught" - Willie wrangles judicial appointment by humble trappings.

"The Hat" - Willie outmaneuvers politician and his advisor.

"Election" - Willie points out insincerity of political candidates.

Stories of the World - Volume 4: Messages from and about Men

Three Brothers (Modified North American Tale) - Brothers illustrate the results of varying personal initiative.

Father and Son at the Hospital (Modified European Tale)- Father shows relationship between level of risk and professional performance.

Two Brothers Inherit a Farm (Modified African Tale) - Shows value of mutual caring and trust.

Stories of the World - Volume 5: In Your Hands

Monkey and the Coconut - monkeys show consequences of personal reactions to circumstances.

Mouse Who Asked What Is It? - curiosity sometimes bring unmanageable consequences.

Old Man and the Eagle - effects of giving others control.

Hunchbacked Prince - prince shows power of personal vision.

Girl Who Ran Away From Home - girl discovers power within.

In Your Hands - shows unexpected wisdom of elders.

Courses and Lectures on Audio Cassette:

Discover Cultural Flexibility: Its Role and Uses as a Concept

Presented by Thomas S. Watson, Jr.
Chairman of Watson Rice International

Global Role for African Americans

Side A - Heritage African American History Month Luncheon Lecture-Explanation of Cultural Flexibility and the competitive edge that African Americans have in a multi-cultural environment. Stories include: "Little Boy Who Left Home"(Modified Japanese Tale).

Side B - Case Western Reserve University, Weatherhead School of Business, Minority Scholars Luncheon Keynote Address. Explains the changing world and offers suggestions of how to properly prepare for a career in the new world. Stories include: "Moses and Mentu" (Modified North American Tale); "Father and Son at the Hospital" (Modified European Tale); "Brothers Who Inherited a Farm" (Modified African Tales)

Discover The New South Africa

Lectures by Thomas S. Watson, Jr., Chairman/Watson Rice International and Jeff van Rooyen, National Director/Deloitte & Touche South Africa (see Chapter on South Africa for Description of Background)

The New South Africa will cause rippling effects across the globe. Let these two pioneers reveal facts and provide advice that you can use to open new career options.

Integration, Comparing Early Experiences

In this revealing series of lectures, Tom Watson and Jeff van Rooyen reveal pioneers' perspectives on integrating business and politics in two great nations. They often wax philosophical when comparing their experiences and the role that unexpected allies have played in making integration possible.

These two bring you a perspective on business, politics and global interdependence that you will not find anywhere else.

How To Protect Your Profits in Government Contracting

by Belinda A. Hogue, CPA and Thomas S. Watson, Jr., CPA, Watson Rice International

This course contains secrets of the government contracting maze. How to Protect Your Profits has been delivered in person more than 75 times by Belinda Hogue and Tom Watson. They have addressed small and medium enterprise audiences assembled by the **Small Business Administration, Department of Defense, local governments and business associations**. Now with their material available on audio cassette and supporting manual, you can benefit from their experience in the comfort of your own office, car or home.

The course contains discussions of:

1. Types of Contracts
2. Developing Cost Proposals
3. Pre-award Accounting and Financial Survey
4. Contract Financing and Payment
5. Contract Close-out

Experience - Together they have:

$ Negotiated multi-million dollar federal contracts for accounting and consulting services. They have also assisted clients in negotiating price and payment terms for many large contracts.

$ Collected payments for scope changes or government induced cost overruns from federal agencies using the "Equitable Adjustment" process.

$ Designed and guided the installation of accounting systems to comply with Federal Acquisition Regulations (FAR) and Cost Accounting Standards.

$ Negotiated financing for federal contracts from banks and other financial institutions.

In response to requests from radio listeners, Tom Watson has released a series of stories on cassettes. These tapes are an up-lifting and entertaining experience. The music makes you tap your foot. They deliver a lasting Spark of Inspiration.

Order Form

Watson Turner Productions, Inc. please send tape(s) to:

Name _____

Title _____

Company _____

Address _____

City/State _____ Zip _____

Tel _____ Fax _____

Stories on Audio Cassette:

Stories of the World:

Volumes 1/2; Africa and Beyond/You Need Oranges

         Quantity _____ @ $10.77 _____ Total

Stories of the World: Volume 3; The Wisdom of Willie

         Quantity _____ @ $ 5.77 _____ Total

Stories of the World: Volume 4; Messages From and About Men

         Quantity _____ @ $ 5.77 _____ Total

Stories of the World: Volume 5; In Your Hands

         Quantity _____ @ $ 5.77 _____ Total

Selected Radio Interviews: Using Stories to Teach Cultural Flexibility

         Quantity _____ @ $ 7.77 _____ Total

Lectures on Audio Cassette: (supporting printed material included)

Global Role for African Americans: 2 lectures

         Quantity _____ @ $17.77 _____ Total

Integrating Politics and Business-lectures (van Rooyen/Watson)

         Quantity _____ @ $17.77 _____ Total

Protecting Profits in Government Contracting (includes supporting manual and references)

         Quantity _____ @ $17.77 _____ Total

The Global Marketplace: Radio interviews with Tom Watson - Free with purchase of a course

Add postage and handling $ 5.00

Total enclosed   ============

  ...Guaranteed full refund of purchase price if you are not completely satisfied...

Make check payable to: Stories/Courses by Tom Watson and mail to:

Tape Order Department
PO Box 34071 Washington, DC 20043
Tel (202)-371-9005; Fax (202)-371-1699; Toll Free (800)-841-2654

Connecting People

Discovering Peace and Power Through Cultural Flexibility

"[His] concepts of cultural flexibility and cultural sensitivity identify the problem and offer a solution, without in any manner lowering standards or sacrificing excellence. Once accepted, learned and understood, our society can and will make meaningful strides toward reaching true cultural diversity." Attorney Robert Preston Brown/Smith, Gambrell & Russell/Atlanta, GA, USA

"Cultural flexibility, as presented through [his] storytelling, is a dynamic concept and disarming to even the most selective listener." Tracey D. Bell, The John F. Kennedy Center for the Performing Arts, Washington, DC, USA

"[I] was enthralled by [his] timely message on Cultural Flexibility. [He] is an excellent storeyteller with an incredible knowledge of international business. He makes issues come alive."; Patricia E. Davis, Case Western Reserve University, Cleveland, OH, USA

Order Form

Nuff Publications please send book(s) to:

Name _____

Title_____ Company_____

Address _____

City/State _____ Zip _____

Tel. _____ Fax _____

Discovering Peace and Power Through Cultural Flexibility

                    Quantity_____ @ $14.95 _____ Total

Add postage and handling $5.00

                            _____

Total enclosed   ===============

Guaranteed full refund of purchase price if you are not completely satisfied

Make check payable to Nuff Publications and mail to:
Thomas S. Watson, Jr.
Department CP 195
Nuff Publications
1010 Vermont Ave., NW, Suite 710
Washington, DC 20005 USA
Tel. (202)-371-9005; Fax (202)-371-1699